The Shadow of DEATH

Kurt A. Vomberg

ISBN 978-1-64258-928-3 (paperback)
ISBN 978-1-64258-969-6 (hardcover)
ISBN 978-1-64258-929-0 (digital)

Copyright © 2018 by Kurt A. Vomberg

All rights reserved. No part of this publication may be reproduced, distributed, or transmitted in any form or by any means, including photocopying, recording, or other electronic or mechanical methods without the prior written permission of the publisher. For permission requests, solicit the publisher via the address below.

Christian Faith Publishing, Inc.
832 Park Avenue
Meadville, PA 16335
www.christianfaithpublishing.com

Printed in the United States of America

To my grandfather who showed me the meaning of love. He gave me guidance and direction. More importantly, he gave me a faith that lasted a lifetime as well as advice that ultimately saved my life.

Foreword

I believe that each of us has a "defining moment." I believe that consciously or unconsciously we prepare for that moment; what we believe in, what we have been taught, and what we are will be put to the ultimate test. How we respond to that challenge will tell us who and what we are, and we will either be at peace with or anguish over that moment for the rest of our lives.

Acknowledgments

First and foremost, I acknowledge Jesus Christ, my Lord and Savior, who spared me and to the Twenty-third Psalm that I repeated innumerable times, giving me strength and courage.

I am grateful to Cheryl McLaughlin who, in the beginning, read my chapters, critiqued, and gave me professional advice.

I need to acknowledge my fellow soldiers and their contributions. Forgive me if some names in the chapters were incorrect. Age and memory loss have fogged some of the details.

I also wish to acknowledge my sister, Theresa, who inspired me and to Alex who made me reflect. Thanks to a community that is unique and special and molded me.

In addition, I want to acknowledge my granddaughter, Haylee, and friend, Janice White, for proofreading and typing the final manuscript.

After Vietnam, I wanted to make my life count for something.

Note: Reference photo credits.

They came from a fellow soldier and a war correspondent, one of which I have been able to recall his name, Specialist 4th Class Israel Romero.

Chapter 1

I read *The Red Badge of Courage* as a boy. Stephen Crane's classic book gets its name from the bloody bandages of the Civil War's wounded soldiers. The story follows a naive young man who goes off to fight. He fantasizes about finding glory, honor, and his manhood on the battlefield.

In his first battle, he experiences the blood and gore of war, and he struggles with his own fear and cowardice. The main character, Henry Fleming, must dig deep within himself to find the courage and bravery to continue as a soldier. Ultimately, he prevails and comes to realize that war is brutal.

The Red Badge of Courage comes to mind when I think about my time in Vietnam.

More than forty years have passed since I went to war. Most of my combat experiences are as clear in my mind as they were the moment that they happened. Yet I buried them for thirty-plus years. I would not let myself talk about them. I wouldn't think about them. I believed that if I was ever to live a normal life, I had to clear my mind of Vietnam and all that happened there. Those memories could not intrude upon my daily life; reliving them would be too painful and too distracting, both emotionally and physically.

I had to lock them away to survive.

Somewhere in the recesses of my mind is a locked room, hidden away at the end of a dark hallway. My Vietnam memories are stored there. On the rare occasions when I open the door, instead of dusty, faded memories, vivid battle scenes play out, and I relive them. Only when I record the scenes on paper do they fade from my memory. Only then can I put them to rest.

It has taken me a lifetime to retrieve those memories bit by bit, record them, and deal with them. I pray for the day when I open that door and the room is empty.

Upon reflection, all I really want is peace—peace with what I had to do, peace with what I'd been through, and peace with what my country told me.

First and foremost, I want peace with what I have done. There are probably as many stories of combat as there are soldiers who survived to tell them. The bottom line is this: in war, it is inevitable there will be a one-on-one engagement and someone will die. I didn't think about killing. It was a reaction to the circumstances. When it was over, I was just grateful to be alive. Every day since my return from Vietnam has been a gift from God. Since then, I've had the love of a wonderful woman, children, grandchildren, and my faith. Unexpectedly, the faces of the dead will wander through my mind from time to time. I know what I have denied them, and that still hurts me.

None of my training prepared me for the brutality of war. I have had the blood, tissue, and pieces of bone from a fellow soldier in my eyes and in my mouth and soaked into my clothes. I have awakened from sleep wringing my hands to wash away the blood that will always be there. I have heard the death rattle in the throat of a dying soldier. I have heard the severely wounded scream for their mothers or begging for God to stop the pain. I have helped load body bags filled with the bodies of soldiers that I knew and who were brothers to me onto helicopters. I have held the shattered body of a fellow soldier in my arms, and I have watched the light in his eyes fade out.

I have seen young men die before they had a chance to live. I believe that God has a special place in heaven for fallen soldiers. He will comfort them, and they will comfort one another. Their souls will finally find peace.

I don't know if I will ever find peace with my country. In fact, I have become increasingly disillusioned over the years. I'm a small-town boy from the Bible Belt, and I was taught that my country was a white knight fighting to save the world from evil wherever it was found. When I was called to military service, I answered the call just as the generations before me had done. I was told we were fighting the spread of communism, and I believed and trusted my country and its leaders. But I lost that trust when our president and congressional leaders caved in to the antiwar coalition. The United States never lost a major battle in the Vietnam War, but my country quit and went home anyway.

Likewise, our leaders disregarded and ignored the nation's commitment to American soldiers. As soldiers, our commitment and our sacrifice never wavered. Yet we were never treated with the same respect that other war veterans received. Who do the families of the more than fifty-six thousand dead and horribly wounded soldiers hold accountable? Who looks these good people in the eye and shoulders the blame? Someone should. The veterans deserve that much!

Part of me believes that I was used and betrayed by my country. I know that you cannot blow the hell out of a country with bombs, kill the majority of its male population, make prostitutes of their women, and then call that democracy. Ultimately, the hardest part for me was to finally admit to myself that the sacrifices we made were in vain and that nobody cared but our families and fellow soldiers. Where and how did we lose our way?

On the other hand, we did protect the South Vietnamese people, at least for a while. Most of them were a kind, gentle people. We delayed their eventual slaughter by the North Vietnamese.

Some in my generation vowed to question authority. I didn't at the time, but I have taught and will continue to teach my grandchildren to question our country's motives and decisions. Likewise, I have advised and will continue to advise them to think long and hard before they commit to military service. My five-year-old grandson comes into my study to see the box of medals that I received from my service in Vietnam. I am concerned about his attachment to these medals. When I finish this story and unearth these memories to set myself free, I will bury the medals under an oak tree in the front yard of my ranch, never to be seen again.

I will grieve for those who never made it home, for my fellow soldiers and friends until the day that I die. Even though the war has long been over, it will always be with me.

Oh, my soul! Let me be whole again. Give me peace!

Chapter 2

The story of my upbringing sounds like the ideal American life from the mid-twentieth century.

I was born in the middle of America in Dodge City, Kansas, in 1945 and raised thirty-seven miles away in Kinsley. It claimed 1,500 citizens, and about the same number lived in the country on farms and ranches. I had two younger sisters. They were both good girls, and I thought the world of them. My dad was the Edwards County sheriff, and he had been voted the toughest sheriff in the state of Kansas by his fellow sheriffs. He had a real presence, and when he talked, I listened.

My mom worked for one of the just three doctors in town. She kept the cleanest house in Kinsley.

I deeply loved and respected my parents. But my grandfather, Frederick Calvert Strate, played the most influential role in my life. My favorite place to spend time was on my grandfather's ranch.

It was a cattle ranch about ten miles outside of town. I got my first horse when I was twelve, and I kept him at Grandpa's ranch. I rode that horse all over the place and used him when we were working cattle branding, dehorning, and vaccinating. I loved it there. I thought I was a cowboy.

When Grandpa did not have me working, he let me hunt anywhere on the ranch that I wanted. I got my first shotgun when I was twelve. I spent hours walking fence rows and plum thickets. Weeds and grass grew tall in the fence rows because the cattle could not graze there. This made a great place for rabbits, pheasants, and quail to hide. I would start at one end of a fence row and walk to the other end. The game would move just ahead of me. The grass and weeds were so thick that I couldn't see what was there. On rare occasions, I would catch a glimpse of something moving through the brush. My excitement would build, and my senses would become more alert as I drew close to the end of the fence row because I never knew what was going to flush out. On one such occasion, as I was drawing close to the end of the row, I remember wondering if the game sensed what was about to happen. If so, what did being hunted feel like?

It would not be the only time I would think about the feeling of being hunted.

Kinsley was a typical tiny town. There were no traffic jams, no air pollution, and no illegal drugs where I grew up. The only thing I knew about drugs was about a weed that grew wild in the pastures and if the cattle ate it, they went crazy. It was known as "loco weed." Years later, I would find out that it was marijuana. If there was any racism in town, I didn't know about it. And if there had been, I didn't experience it. I had friends who were Mexican and African American, and we all got along just fine.

I was pretty typical, too. Football, basketball, and hunting were my passions in Kinsley. At 7 p.m. on an autumn Friday night, just about everyone was at the high school football field watching the game. We all knew everyone's name, and everyone went to church on Sunday.

My maternal grandparents were Southern Baptists, and on alternate Sundays, I was in church with them. I went forward in the church when I was twelve and was baptized in a sand pit at nineteen as a believing adult. My father was Catholic, and on the Sundays when I was not in the Baptist church, I was at mass with him. I went through Catechism at age ten and had my first communion. I was in one church or the other every Sunday. There were things I liked in both churches and things I questioned. Ultimately, I learned to go to the Bible with my questions, and I would find the answer that I was seeking. But both churches were guilty of putting their own spin on Christianity.

I thought school was great. I got to play sports and see pretty girls every day. I enjoyed most of my classes, and I did all right. Most of my schoolwork came easily to me. When I went away to college,

I missed my family and friends, but I adapted to college life quickly. I joined Sigma Phi Epsilon fraternity and thought that life could not get much better. I was halfway through when one day, after a late-night party and hangover, I started to think about what I wanted to do with my life. I was fine academically, making grades and all. My life was one party after another and one girl after another. I never thought about getting married, settling down, and having children. I knew that I could have and should have been getting a lot more out of my college education. If I stayed in school and finished my degree, I would get drafted right after graduation.

This was a dilemma. It would be difficult to find a job after two or three years in the military. I would have to go back to college to get a job. I decided that I should enlist in the military and complete my obligation. After I was discharged, I would return to college on the GI Bill and get my degree. My military service would be behind me, and I could find a career and be set. I had a life plan.

I looked to my grandfather for guidance in all things. He was truly a man for all seasons. A graduate of Pittsburg State College in Kansas, he was the smartest man that I knew. He was a teacher and a coach before becoming a full-time rancher. He read three newspapers every day of his life until he died at age ninety-two. He was a devout Southern Baptist and a very conservative Democrat, but his faith came first.

Grandpa would drive his old pickup truck to town Friday afternoon to pick me up from school and take me to the ranch for the weekend and on holidays. On our way back to the ranch, he would also become my teacher too, pointing out different flowers, shrubs, and trees to tell me all of their names. In the country, he would point out the different breeds of cattle and horses, as well as various crops. He gave me a complete description of whatever he saw. I was amazed with his knowledge. He also took advantage of this private time to lecture me on the evils of alcohol, tobacco, and "loose women." He quoted both scripture and poetry with equal eloquence. He had a way of explaining things that made them make sense. He was a tough taskmaster, and he always demanded my best effort.

I didn't know it at the time, but one of those lectures would save my life.

When I had finished my military training, my orders sent me to the Republic of South Vietnam. I remember that it was our last week of training and we were standing in formation as our company commander called us to attention. I can still hear his words: "The following soldiers have been selected to report to the Republic of South Vietnam. You've been taught to kick ass and take names. You are ready. Good luck and keep your head down."

Mine was the third name called.

I'm used to being called last. My last name begins with a V, and all through school, mine was always just about the last name called. I was surprised and caught off guard at being called third. After our last week of training, we were given thirty days' leave to visit our loved ones before shipping out. That's when I got to see Grandpa.

We got together for one of our talks. Actually, he talked; I listened. He had a way of teaching life lessons that made them stick. He told me that the Bible said that there was a time to beat the plow shear into a sword. He told me that during the prayer service at our Baptist church at 7 p.m. every Tuesday night, they would all be praying for me.

Here's the important part. He told me to go over what I might have to do in my mind and that I had to be crystal clear in my mind how I would react because any hesitation on my part could get me killed.

"Make sure your heart is right with God, "he said. Then he handed me a pocket Bible. I carried it in my breast pocket all the time I was in Vietnam.

Many years after my grandfather died, my mother told me that Grandpa had figured out that I would probably be getting up at 6 a.m. in Vietnam or 4 a.m. Kansas time. Grandpa got up at 4 a.m. every day to pray for me that year I was in Vietnam.

Chapter 3

Soldiers were given thirty days of leave before reporting for duty in Vietnam. When my thirty days were up, my family took me to Mid-Continent Airport in Wichita, Kansas. It was a tearful goodbye, and I could see the stress in my mother's face. From Wichita, I flew to a military base in San Francisco. Once in San Francisco, I caught a cab to the military base, where I checked in, and I was assigned to a Quonset hut barracks. There were armed military police guarding the door. No one could leave the barracks. I guess they wanted to make sure that no one changed his mind about going to Vietnam. We were fed in the barracks, and it even had a wet bar where we could buy pitchers of beer. There was a jukebox next to the bar, and the most popular song was "Snoopy and the Red Baron." It was as close to a war song as we could get, and it was played over and over again. Everybody sang and laughed. It was our last night in the United States for a year. The next day, we would be off to an unforeseen future. The next morning, we were loaded onto buses and taken to the airport. Again, armed military police marched us from the barracks to the buses. They even rode with us to the airport. At the airport, 130 GIs were loaded onto a plane. Ironically, they were commercial planes, not military. Delta Airlines delivered me to the Vietnam War. The only good thing about the flight was that back then, the stewardesses still had to be attractive. We flew from San Francisco toward a seacoast city in Japan. We had been on the plane for many hours, and it was pitch black outside. After we landed, we deplaned to stretch and get a little exercise.

The first thing I noticed was the smell. It was hot, and the stench was almost overwhelming. Guys were throwing up because the smell was so bad. We were glad to get back on the plane to escape that horrible smell.

We landed in Camron Bay, Vietnam, eight hours later. When I stepped out of the plane into the Vietnam air, it felt like I had just stepped into an oven. I had never felt heat this intense before. I was instantly drenched in sweat.

Camron Bay was a reception area located on a bay of the same name. All new incoming GIs had to process through Camron. We spent four days there reviewing information that we had already been through. The last thing that we were told was to which Army unit we were assigned. On the fifth day, we left Camron for our units. My designation was the An Khe base camp of the First Cavalry Division. An Khe was in the central highlands in Gia Lai Province. From mid-1965 to 1968, it was base camp for the 1st Calvary Infantry Division.

We flew from Camron Bay to An Khe in an Air Force C-130 cargo plane. As the C-130 circled An Khe for landing, I got my first glimpse of base camp through the plane window. The first thought that came to my mind was that it looked like a fort in the middle of the jungle, and it was. The base camp was a rectangle with the airfield in the middle. All along, the outside perimeter of the base camp was row after row of barbed wire. Every hundred yards along the perimeter were bunkers made of steel frames that were covered with sandbags. Inside each bunker were two soldiers who manned a machine gun. Extending from the barbed wire about two hundred yards, all of the vegetation was gone. There was nothing but dirt. I learned later that the area was called the kill zone. The vegetation had been chopped, sprayed, burned, and plowed flat by bulldozers. The military mindset was if the enemy tried to mass a ground attack, they would have to cross two hundred yards of open ground. Machine guns and rifle fire from the bunkers would make this a slaughter or at least a heavy casualty situation.

Seeing the base camp was a reality check. This was the face of war. A thousand thoughts raced through my mind. I was excited to be there, yet I wondered how it would turn out for me. This is what I had been trained for.

There were about forty of us who got off the C-130. A sergeant got us into formation, called out our names, and told us what companies we were assigned to. Three of us and our duffle bags were loaded into a jeep and taken to our company area. Our next stop was the orderly room, which was the command center for the company. It contained the office of the first sergeant, the ranking noncommissioned officer commonly referred to as Top, and the company commander, the ranking commissioned officer referred to as the Old Man. The first sergeant handed the Old Man my DD214 file, which contained my personal records. That file had the results of my battery of military tests, my IQ score, scores and ratings from basic and advanced training, scores from weapon ranges, physical training tests, and my education level. I had qualified with every weapon in the US Army's arsenal from a 45-caliber pistol to the main gun on a tank and every caliber of weapon in between. I qualified as an expert with all of them.

Maybe all that hunting in Kansas had paid off.

When you report to your company commander for the first time, there is a protocol. You march into the office and stop directly in front of his desk. You come to the position of attention and state your name, rank, and serial number. You fix your eyes straight ahead on the wall behind him. You are locked into the position of attention while the Old Man looks you over. He will eventually get around to giving you the "at ease" command, which is your cue to relax. He never said a word as he opened my file. He slowly leafed through the pages.

Finally, he looked up at me and said, "Son, says here that you are a college boy. Is that true?"

My response was a, "Yes, sir," in a loud, strong voice, the way we were taught in training.

He continued. "Says here you scored a perfect score on the rifle range. Says here you're 6 foot 5 and weigh 225 pounds, and it says here you're an athlete. All these true, son?"

"Yes, sir."

"Congratulations, son. You are the new point man for my scout team. The first sergeant will explain to you what a point man does. Now, get the hell out of my office."

From the Old Man's office, I was taken to "the hooch," which was the barracks where I would live when I was in base camp. There were twenty soldiers living in the hooch. The hooch was divided in half with a walkway down the middle and ten men on each side. Each soldier had a cot, a wall locker, and a footlocker. The inside of the hooch was made out of a two-by-four wooden frame. There was a thick, heavy canvas tent stretched over the wood frame. From the floor rising four feet along the outside wall were row after row of sandbags. The sandbags were there to protect the GIs from shrapnel and mortar attacks. The inside of the hooch was clean and neat. The soldiers wore clean starched fatigues. They were bathed, clean-shaven with a high tight haircut and were disciplined in appearance and conduct. The morale, professionalism, and pride that I heard about were evident in the ranger outfits. It was much more than I expected. These soldiers were the best of the best, and I was impressed. Esprit de Corps defined them.

I was given my own area in the hooch with a cot, a wall locker, and a footlocker to stow my gear. I was about halfway through when a second lieutenant came up to me and introduced himself as my platoon leader. He was young but impressive. He looked like a college quarterback. He told me that the Old Man was serious about me being the new point man. He told me that the life expectancies for an infantry second lieutenant and the point man were about the same—relatively short. We laughed. There was nothing else we could do.

The lieutenant explained to me that the point man walked about thirty yards ahead of the rest of the team. The point man was the eyes and ears of the team. He explained the fact that me being tall gave me a greater field of vision. I was told that whenever my team moved, I would be out front. He didn't say anything about me being the first target that the enemy would see. He didn't have to.

For the next five days that I was in base camp, I was told what my job was and how to do it. I was fine with the weapons and the tactics, but I needed a refresher course on maps and compass coordination. I was loaded into a chopper and transported to the team's location. It was my first time in a helicopter, and it was exciting.

The pilot told me to keep my head down entering and exiting the chopper.

"The blade will take off the head of a tall person," he said.

He also explained that when he got to the landing zone (LZ), he wasn't going to land. He would do a "touch and go." That means he would drop to about four feet above the ground, and he expected me to jump while he was still moving forward. Coming to a complete stop could make him an easy target. Everything about the flight was exciting. The helicopter was noisy, and it would blow any loose dirt, leaves and twigs, or other debris into the air. The faster the rotation of the rotor blades as they built up speed for the takeoff, the more debris blew into the air.

Finally, he had enough speed to lift, and he pulled the helicopter up and away. When we reached the altitude he wanted, he leveled off. Everything below us was many shades of green. I would come to enjoy the time up there. We were above the bullets and the madness for a few precious moments.

We were headed for the rim which formed the top of the hill that defined one side of the valley into which we were about to descend. The pilot dropped the chopper over the top into rapid descent toward the bottom of the valley. We were almost at the bottom of the valley when the pilot pointed to a small open area. He dropped me there.

The three-man scout team was somewhere on this side of the valley. A soldier came out of the grass. He said two things to me.

"Let's go," and, "keep up."

We moved fast, and we were going straight uphill. He stopped a couple of times to take out his binoculars and to check behind us. We got to our position about an hour before dark. The team had dug three foxholes. They handed me an entrenching tool and showed me where to dig my foxhole.

A foxhole should be large enough to have your entire body fit inside. By the time I got my foxhole dug, it was dark. I had a week's supply of c-rations back at camp. I took a box from my rucksack. It held a p-38, a miniature can opener. I used it to begin opening the cans. It was so dark that I couldn't read anything on the cans, so

I opened the first can and ate the contents. It was terrible. Later, I figured it out. I was eating a can of beef stew, and the top half inch was nothing but lard.

That night, I was told we had two guys on guard and two sleeping. We rotated every two hours. The next day happened to be my birthday. I spent the day filling sandbags, fine-tuning my foxhole to make it bigger, and cleaning my weapon.

Every birthday since then has been a gift. I always reflect and say a prayer of thanks.

The team leader was strange. He had blond hair, his complexion was fair and red tinged, and he had the coldest blue eyes I had ever seen. I had never met anyone who made me feel like he could kill me in a heartbeat. There was something cold and threatening about him. He was from Cleveland, Ohio. A city boy shouldn't have had the instincts of a jungle cat that he had. He moved quietly, quickly, and his head and eyes were constantly moving from side to side. He was well built. He was an Airborne Ranger, and his training had allowed for great physical condition. He was also the first soldier whom I had trouble keeping up with. Little by little, he would talk about ambush patrols (AP) and listening patrols (LP). The experiences of killing and almost being killed had made him what he needed to be to survive. The difference was that I believed he had begun to enjoy the experience.

The first thing he said was, "Forget everything you've been told and listen to me if you want to stay alive."

The next thing he said was, "Sleep on guard and I will kill you." He proceeded to tell me to dump out the contents of my rucksack. He took my T-shirts, socks, boxers, toothpaste, and deodorant and told me to dig a hole and bury them. He told me that the T-shirts, socks, and boxers would hold sweat and rain and rot from my body. He told me the NVA (North Vietnamese Army) would smell the toothpaste and deodorant.

I stayed on that side of the mountain for five days. We watched as the NVA moved into the valley. We had a PRC-25 two-way radio, and the team leader called in the air strikes. After all the air strikes, he would take the other two soldiers and go down to check out what was left. They would leave me alone on the mountain. It was my job to watch the valley and make sure that no one came up behind them. When he returned, he would call in the casualty reports and the patches and documents that he had removed from the dead soldiers to take back to Army intelligence. I looked at the patches and documents and couldn't help thinking that hours before these were in the possession of live soldiers. One time I heard the rifle fire. When the team came back, they didn't talk about it; I didn't ask. But when the team leader talked on the radio, I would hear bits and pieces of what had taken place.

The morning of the sixth day, we came down from the mountain. The chopper picked us up and took us back to base camp. The sergeant may have been psycho, but I learned a lot in those five days. Every day spent in base camp was a day that was looked at as a vacation. You could sleep at night on a cot. You could take a shower and get a hot meal. We were in the base camp for three days when on the morning of the fourth day, our company loaded onto choppers about an hour before daylight. We headed back to the "Happy Valley," a nickname given to the area by one of the soldiers.

We were called an assault group. Our company had a little over a hundred soldiers. Ten soldiers would load onto each chopper. We flew in a V formation. About a mile from the village, we hit the LZ. The choppers touched the ground, and we bailed out. It was just turning daylight, and it was foggy. We lined up in a straight line and were told we would move quickly and quietly toward the village.

When we got there, the fog had almost burned off. There was smoke from the cooking fires and a strong smell of fish. I was walking straight toward a grass hut. When I was about thirty yards away, a dog came out through the open door. At about twenty yards from the hut, I saw a figure stand. It was dark inside the hut and hard for me to see. I continued to walk toward the door; the figure also approached the door. He was naked from the waist up. His trousers were NVA khaki combat fatigues. Our eyes met, and I could see the surprise on his face. He reached above his head with his right arm to the top of the door. He was frantically trying to grasp his rifle. I saw the stock of the rifle first. My first bullet hit him in the biceps.

I could see the muscle tissue explode. The impact of my bullet spun him into the rest of my burst which caught him across the upper chest. I could see the blood spraying from the bullet holes in his chest. He fell backward. I walked up to the door and looked inside the hut. He had been alone. I bent down and picked up his rifle and threw it outside. Then I looked into his eyes; he was gasping for breath that would not come. He wasn't quite dead.

I watched him die.

I looked at his lifeless body and thought, "So this is the way, kill or be killed." There is nothing in between. After all these years, my hand still shakes as I write this.

We went through the village and found ten more NVA soldiers. Another dozen tried to flee from the other side of the village. They were cut down by the gunship flying support overhead. The thing I learned that day is that it only takes three pounds of pressure on a trigger to kill. Pulling the trigger was the easy part. The tough part was living with the consequences. For more than forty years, the faces have never left me, and I never know when one will wander through my mind.

A chopper came in and picked up our recon team and took us to a new location. Ordinarily, we would go back to base camp for a few days before we were sent back out into the boonies. Not this time. We were briefed on our way to the new location. We knew this had to be important because we weren't given any down time and the last thing we were told before they dropped us off was there was heavy enemy activity in the area.

We were dropped off in the bottom of the valley. We immediately moved about halfway up the side of the mountain. For five hours, until it got dark, we moved toward our new checkpoint. We moved through this valley for three days. Halfway into the second day, I experienced an uneasiness that I had never experienced before. That uneasiness never left me. I knew there was something bad out there and that it was close.

Halfway through the fourth day, we decided to make an arc and come back to our trail to see if we were being followed. We spent the entire day there and saw nothing. We spent the night there, too, and part of the next morning until we moved out. By early afternoon, we could hear a waterfall in the distance. The closer we got, the louder it got. The waterfall noise blocked sounds we would normally have heard. Before we got to the top of the knoll near the falls, we spread out and dropped to our bellies. We low crawled to the top of the knoll and peered down to the waterfall below. There were four NVA soldiers next to the waterfall. They were a recon team operating in the same area that we were. Here was the source of my uneasiness. My instincts were telling me something that my eyes now confirmed.

They had made a fire and were cooking food. We retreated down the knoll and gathered together. The plan was that our team leader would go all the way down the knoll and come in on the left bank. The third member of our team was to go down the knoll and circle around on the right bank. I was to go back to the top of the knoll and watch the NVA. If they tried to leave, I was to open fire, but our goal was to take at least one of them prisoner.

When I got back to the top of the knoll, I looked down on the NVA. They were sitting around the fire eating and talking. I remember thinking what a beautiful place this was. The falls shot out of a wall that was two hundred feet tall. The face of the falls was sheer and covered in green tropical plants. It looked like a huge, thick, green carpet. The water fell into a rock basin. It looked like a big swimming pool. Over many years, the falling water had carved out and polished the pool. The water was crystal clear.

When the NVA finished eating, one of them rolled a joint, and they passed it around until it was gone. Then they took off all of their clothes and jumped into the pool. I envied them. They were having a good time. The NVA made a critical mistake. They all jumped in the pool. They should have left one man on watch.

From my vantage point above them, I could see the other two members of our team moving in. The NVA couldn't see them because the pool was four feet below ground level.

When they were about twenty yards from the NVA weapons and clothes, I stood up and started down the knoll. I made it all the way down the knoll before they saw me. Even from a distance, I could see the terror in their eyes. They knew that they were about to die. The three of us walked about fifteen feet to the edge of the ledge where the NVA had jumped into the water. The seven of us stared at each other for several seconds. Finally, one of the NVA separated himself from the other three and swam straight for us even though their weapons were piled behind us. I have often wondered what he was thinking coming at us that way. He had heart.

When he was about five yards from us, our team leader put a burst of fire into him. Red streams of blood poured from his body. He splashed around for a while, and then his lifeless body sank to the bottom of the pool. Two of the three NVA left immediately dove to the bottom of the pool and grabbed rocks to anchor themselves. I motioned the third NVA to come to the side of the pool. He would be our prisoner.

The other two team members started shooting bursts into the water at the two NVA who were anchored to the bottom of the pool. This was like shooting fish in a barrel, an execution. I didn't take part. I couldn't kill in cold blood. I knew that they had to die, and I knew if the tables were turned, our fate would be much worse. Yet it was gruesome to watch. I took control of the prisoner. He was no problem. He was grateful to be alive. We called in for our pickup, got it, and moved out.

Chapter 4

When I was a boy, we had a huge beautiful willow tree in our backyard. I loved to climb and play in it. I could stand underneath it when it was raining and not get wet. On days when it was sunny and hot, I could sit in the shade of this tree, and it would feel twenty degrees cooler. Underneath this willow tree was a brick patio with a picnic table. I would go into the backyard after dark. I would take a flashlight, sit at the picnic table, and listen to the sounds of the night. I would focus on one sound and try to figure out what was making it. Then, I would isolate where the sound was coming from and turn the flashlight toward the sound to see what was making it.

After a while, I didn't have to turn the flashlight on at all. I knew if the noise was a locust, a tree frog, a cricket, or whatever else it possibly could be. I learned to be comfortable with the sounds of the night. I understood and appreciated them for what they were, but the lesson I learned that helped me the most was when the noise stopped, a predator had come into the area.

I used that skill in Vietnam.

After the village in the Happy Valley, we went immediately back to base camp. I knew that the day in the village had changed me. I felt my mind began to build calluses, and I started suppressing my emotions. I would not allow myself to think about it. Killing and death became a reality for me that day.

We had been in camp for a short period of time when the word came that our recon team was going out with a battalion on a search-and-destroy mission. We would be our battalion's eyes and ears. One of the guys on the four-man team had thirty days left on his year-long tour of duty in Vietnam, which meant that he got to stay in camp. He was not going out with the team.

We were taken out in a chopper and dropped off in the area that would become the LZ for the battalion. It was our job to recon the area. I spent the next twenty-four hours moving in a circle, watching and listening. We gradually increased the size of the circle, but we found no signs of the enemy. The next day, the battalion hit the LZ and it was cold, which meant that no shots had been fired at our soldiers or our helicopters. We had done our job.

There were three more recon teams in addition to ours. Every night we could go out on a listening post (LP), and every fourth day we went out on an ambush post (AP). The battalion would spread out and move all day. Then about an hour before dark, they would stop for the day and set up a perimeter. When we went out, we would get our orders from the battalion commander. We would do our best to get to our assigned location before dark. You would get a better feel for what was around you, like the grass, bamboo, and trees. If you could see it in the daylight, then you could put a game plan together.

When we went out, we had a map, a compass, a flashlight, and a spot on the map. We had a PRC-25 radio, but once we left the battalion, we didn't talk. Every fifteen minutes, we "broke squelch," which was a soft, scratchy sound, once if everything was okay, twice if we made contact with the enemy, and three times if the shit had hit the fan. There were many critical techniques involved in what we were doing, but the number one thing was to know how to read the map and how to be where we were supposed to be on time. We would call in artillery for strikes, and we did not want them coming down on us. When the first artillery round hit, the enemy would know that we were some place in the area. If the artillery barrage came in on top of them, they would not have time to look for us. If it missed, they did.

On an LP, we would be sent to a spot away from the main body of our soldiers, and we would stay there all night to listen and observe. We would find a spot where we could see but not be seen. We would put out our claymore mines. They were shaped like bananas, and they were about two inches thick, five inches wide, and about ten inches long. They were filled with C-4, a plastic explosive, and buck shot, a small steel shot about half the size of a pea. They both sat on two small, fold-down tripods that brought them down to about four inches off the ground. They were operated by fifty feet of slender wire. On one end of the wire was the firing mechanism, and on the other was an electrode that screwed into the C-4. Claymores could kill out to fifty feet in front of them and about ten feet behind them. We stayed in this position from dusk until dawn. We took turns sleeping, but two of us would always be awake with one man sleeping. We were there to be eyes and ears but not to engage the enemy. We could call in artillery. Once the artillery started, we would leave the area quickly.

Ambushes were totally different. The purpose of an ambush was to bring back a prisoner.

We had two types of enemy soldiers. The Viet Cong were local farmers and villagers. They would drop a couple of mortars on us and be home in time for supper. For the most part, they had little training and didn't wear uniforms. The NVA was well trained and wore uniforms. They were our target and they were brutal. A squad of four or five soldiers was what we were looking for. We would find a heavily traveled trail. Then we would attach a claymore mine approximately head high to a tree with the killing part facing into the tree. We would set off the claymores in the middle of them as they would walk down the trail. One or two would survive the blast, and we would take them prisoner. Since they were so disoriented from the ambush, they usually didn't resist. The one thing that I know about the Vietnam War was that we treated Vietnamese prisoners a lot better than they treated the American prisoners.

It was common knowledge among the American soldiers that the NVA did not take wounded prisoners. Any soldier below the rank of lieutenant was tortured and then executed. We never forgot that. When our battalion went on search and destroy, missions could last from one week to two months or longer. The objective was to clear a particular area of all enemy activity. Day by day, I was gaining experience. I could handle what we were doing. Some of what we did I enjoyed and got a rush.

I had been out on an operation for about five weeks when I was airlifted by medevac for the first time. I was put on a medevac chopper to the 93rd Evacuation Hospital in Long Binh. When I look back on those five weeks, two distinct incidents are still with me.

In the first incident, we got to our position on the map a little late. I don't know if the enemy saw us coming or if they had heard us. We got to our position about fifteen minutes before dark, and soon we could hear the enemy talking. They started to probe us. We were in elephant grass close to the edge of the jungle. We heard their voices, and we began to move away from them. That was exactly what they had wanted us to do.

They opened fire on us.

We hit the ground and low crawled our way back to the elephant grass that we had just left. We dropped a couple of claymore mines and moved in a different direction. We had gone about a hundred yards when they decided to open up on us again. So we decided to turn around and go back. We received the same fire. We knew that we were surrounded. We crawled our way back to the center and called for help, giving our coordinates. We were told that a gunship would be near us in twenty minutes. We started crawling low again, this time through the grass toward the trees of the jungle. Enemy bullets tore the grass down and threw grass and dirt into the air. We could see the barrel flashes from the AK-47s. The circle was being saturated with bullets. Two of the NVA soldiers started coming toward us with their guns blazing. We set off claymores, and I heard the men scream. The dust and the dirt that was in the air from the explosion gave us the distraction we needed to get to the trees. It also gave us some valuable time.

We got a call from the gunship saying that it was two minutes away. The man on the radio told us that when he was above us to pop a smoke grenade and find cover quickly. He told us that he would clear a path from the smoke grenade northward.

Finally, we could hear the gunship. As directed, we waited until he was right above us. We threw the smoke grenade as far away from us as we could. It was like something out of a science fiction movie. I was standing behind a tree looking over a forked branch. It all began with a high-pitched scream. The chopper pilot stood the helicopter on its nose and opened fire. It looked like a stream of fire coming out of the helicopter. When it hit the ground, it sounded as if a million bees had been released. Dirt and debris filled the air. The pilot flew the chopper in a zigzag pattern back and forth. A five-second burst from a gunship would put at least one bullet in every square inch of an area the size of a football field. Everything was shredded by the bullets, and the debris in the air made it hard to breathe. He cleared one hundred yards for us, and we took off on a dead run through the cleared breach. The next day, we went back to the same area with the battalion and found the bodies of eighteen men.

The chopper pilot had saved our lives.

During my year in Vietnam, I experienced fear many times, but only once was it almost overwhelming. After all these years, every now and then, I wake up in a cold sweat, always from remembering this experience in my dreams. We had gone out on an LP. We went into a tall, thick clump of elephant grass and continued to set up. We ran our claymores around us in a circle. I made a small visual lane in the grass so I could see out. There was almost a full moon, which meant the light made it easy to see. There were three of us sitting on the ground with our backs touching. At about two in the morning, I was looking up at the stars trying to see the Big Dipper. Suddenly, the night creature sounds stopped. I looked out in front of me, and a single NVA soldier was walking through. He was a scout or point man for a group of soldiers that would be coming after him. I had been through this before, and it had my full attention. Immediately, I became fully alert. Two minutes went by, and three more NVA soldiers came past us. They were lined up abreast of each other with fifty-yard intervals between them. I had seen this before as well, so I knew it would be a good sized unit.

Two more minutes went by, but instead of a squad or platoon of NVA, six NVA came through us lined up abreast with fifty-yard gaps between them. I had never seen this many scouts come through in advance before. I knew that we were going to see a lot more NVA soldiers than we had ever seen. One more group of scouts came through. I stopped counting at ten. They were in line with fifty-yard intervals. When they passed through, I checked to make sure the other two men next to me were awake. None of the NVA scouts had come within thirty yards of us. They were moving fast, wherever they were going. They wanted to be there before daylight.

A couple of minutes later, as I looked through my hole in the grass, a wall of NVA soldiers were moving toward us. My heart was pounding. I had never seen this many NVA soldiers. My mind was racing. Should I open up on them? Should I set off the claymores? Should I run? It was too late. They were on top of us. I watched them walk right at us.

Then they swerved around the tall clump of grass where we were hiding. They came so close to me that I was afraid one of them would step on me. My heart was pounding so hard that it was like a drum beating in my ears. I thought they would hear it. They walked by us for what seemed like a lifetime. Had one of us moved, if one of them had walked through the clump of tall grass, or had one of them tripped over or saw the wire from one of our claymores, we all would have been dead.

I could smell the fish and the fire smoke on them. I could have reached out and touched them. They walked through us for twenty minutes. It was the longest twenty minutes of my life. When it was over, I could not believe that we had survived. At least 1,500 NVA soldiers had walked through us.

We waited five minutes and then called in artillery strikes. We started running as the artillery rounds started coming in on the NVA. We had been running for about five minutes when something exploded behind me. I remember flying through the air and hitting the ground face first. I got up and shook my head. My ears were ringing, and I was dizzy. The back of my legs were wet and burning. I started running again. We made it back to the base camp two long hours later. My ears were still ringing from the explosion, and I had come to find out that the moisture and burning in the back of my legs were from shrapnel. They put me on a chopper and sent me to the 93rd Evacuation Hospital. I did not know it at the time, but I would not be sent back to the First Cavalry Division when I was released from the hospital. I would be reassigned to the Recon Platoon 2nd and 34th Armor.

On occasion, I still wake up in a cold sweat with my heart racing, and I relive this experience!

Chapter 5

The years have come and gone, and it still bothers me to go into a hospital. I get flashbacks, and it's almost like the physical pain comes back to my body.

When they brought me into the 93rd, I didn't have any life-threatening wounds, but I was messed up. My ears felt like they were full of water, and they never stopped ringing. The back of my calves and thighs had multiple shrapnel wounds. The pieces were small but pierced deep. Most of them they dug out, but some were too deep. The doctor told me that eventually they would work their way to the surface. He was right, but he didn't tell me some would still be there several years later.

I liked to take long hot showers and then switch to cold water. My flesh cooled faster than the metal. I could tell where the metal was because it stayed hot and I could feel it. Eventually, it would work its way to the surface, and I could dig it out with my fingernails. The ringing in my ears turned into an infection, and I lost my equilibrium. I couldn't even stand up. I was put on an antibiotic. It worked, but they kept me for about a week and a half in the hospital.

I was smart enough to realize every day in the hospital was one less day in combat, and I was grateful for that.

We got three hot meals a day and a good night's sleep. The best part was that the nurses were American girls, and they had been the first I had seen in two months. The pain medications they had me on put me in a fog. I drifted in and out of consciousness for the first five days. But I did get a lot of sleep which I needed badly.

Gradually, as they began to wean me off the pain medication, my head became clear. I started to realize what was going on around me. Now that I look back on it, I must have been in an amputee ward. The soldier on the left was missing his left arm from the elbow down. He would take his right hand and put it on his left shoulder. There he would slowly move his hand down his arm to the elbow. He would feel for the rest of his arm that wasn't there. He did this over and over again hoping that he was wrong or that somehow the outcome would change.

I made a couple of attempts to talk to him, but he never responded. He was in his own world.

The soldier on my right lost his right leg from the knee down. He didn't talk, and he moved very little. He had been there a few days, and I remember something began to smell. It was faint at first, but then it became stronger. I asked the nurse what it was, and she looked away but didn't answer. Later she brought a doctor. He removed the bandages from the soldier's other leg. Then, they left the room without speaking. Right after lunch, they came and got him. The next time I saw him, he was missing both of his legs. He was so medicated that he barely moved. On the third day, I heard him crying. He had come out from under the medication and realized that he lost his other leg.

The lights in the hospital were very dim. The smells except for the nurses' perfume were bad. Soldiers would wake everyone up with their screams during the night. The clearer my mind got, the more depressing the hospital became. I was ready to leave and go back to my unit.

Two days later, I was given some antibiotics and pain pills, and then I was released. A jeep picked me up and took me to an airfield.

The irony was that I believe that the round, either artillery or mortar, was friendly fire that fell short.

It was seven months later when I was wounded for the second time. We were on a "search-and-destroy" mission, and the track next to me hit mine. The blast from it hit my track and me. The blast slammed me into my steel machine gun shield.

I really didn't remember anything until I woke in the hospital. Later, after I was released from the hospital and sent back to my unit, I found out what had happened. One of the soldiers on the track next to me told me that the blast almost turned my track over. It slammed the left side of my head and left shoulder. He told me that I was knocked unconscious when they found me and remained unconscious when they loaded me onto the medevac chopper.

When I woke up, I was told that I was in the 45th Surgical Hospital in Chew Ly. They couldn't or wouldn't tell me anything about what had happened to the rest of my crew.

The hospital was located on the ocean at the end of an airfield. From what I could see, the airfield consisted mostly of Marine fighter jets, Army C-130 cargo planes, and a squadron of helicopters. They flew over the hospital on landings and take offs, which made no sense to me.

When I woke up, I had one hell of a headache, my ears were ringing, and all of the muscles between my left shoulder and the left side of my head felt like they were on fire.

The first face I remember was that of a nurse. She looked like an Angel of Mercy to me. I hadn't seen an American in several months.

The first couple of days were pretty much a blur. I was on pain killers, and to add to that, I couldn't hear too much.

Little by little, day by day, I got better. The ringing in my ears began to subside, but the headaches were brutal. The pain I was in would be so bad that I would throw up.

I learned to take my thumbs and put them on my temples where my veins were; when the headaches started, the blood would pound in my veins. I could take my thumbs and push on the veins and shut off the blood flow to my brain. It really made a big difference.

Nothing they gave me worked as good as my thumbs. I would lay there for hours with my thumbs on my temples, sometimes long enough for me to fall asleep. As my thumbs relaxed, it allowed more blood to my brain and more pain. It would wake me up, and I would start the procedure all over again.

The time between the headaches became longer, but they never completely stopped.

The soldier in the bed next to me on the right was a Green Beret. He was out with a recon team. They were walking across some rice paddy dikes when he was hit from behind by a water buffalo.

One of the horns hit him in the buttocks and came out through his thigh. The buffalo continued to run with him impaled on its horn. Finally, the other soldiers in his recon team shot and killed it.

It amazed me. You would see the Vietnamese children leading the water buffalo around by a string through their nose. Docile as could be, but if a soldier got close to them, they would go crazy.

We would kid him about his wound and ask him how he was going to explain the other hole in his ass to his family back home. He had a sense of humor, and it was nice to laugh.

The soldier on the other side of me had a concussion and ear problems from a hand grenade explosion. He could take a drag off a cigarette and blow smoke out of his ears. I swear I saw him do it. The nurses would get onto him about doing it. He'd wait until they would walk away, and he'd do it behind their backs. It would crack us up.

This hospital wasn't nearly as depressing as the 93rd Evac. The soldiers around me were friendly and talkative. We all talked about home and where we came from. We talked about our families and the first thing we would do when we got home. It was nice to be able to relax and laugh. I needed the sleep. The hot meals tasted great after eating c-rations for several months. And we got to take hot showers.

Not having seen an American girl in seven months, I enjoyed listening and talking to the nurses. It was a treat just to look at them and watch them walk.

I'd been there over a week, and the hospital was kind of laid back. That was nice. They must have had a big battle someplace because the hospital filled up and things got hectic.

The new soldiers coming in were in a lot of pain, and they were traumatized. Along with the soldiers came two babies.

I hadn't realized it before, but when I got there, the hospital was at about one-third of capacity. Most of the soldiers had been there for a while, so it was kind of quiet and calm.

Now all of a sudden, everything changed. The nurses and doctors were moving fast and furiously.

At night, the nurses didn't have time to take care of the babies. So they would bring them to us for help.

THE SHADOW OF DEATH

The babies had been brought in from a village. The village had come under mortar attack. No one knew if the mortars were ours or the enemies. I guess it didn't matter. The results were the same.

One of the babies had all of its fingers and thumbs blown off. There was black stitching thread where the fingers and thumbs should have been. The other baby had been split open just above its navel to the top of its breast bone. The wound was a long straight line, and it almost looked like a zipper.

At night the babies would cry, the nurses would bring them to us for help because they were too busy. We would take turns holding them and rocking them. We learned how to do it right because if they cried, the other soldiers couldn't sleep.

In the mornings, the babies would have puss in their eyes, and the nurses taught us how to take cotton balls to clean their eyes.

I guess the good thing about helping with these babies was it made us realize that we didn't have it so bad after all.

I spent another week in the hospital before I was sent back to my unit. A jeep came and picked me up and took me over to the airfield. There was an Air Force load master with a clipboard.

He was standing next to the C-130 that we were supposed to leave on. They had dropped the back deck on the C-130. For three hours, they pulled jeeps, trucks, and equipment into the C-130 and secured it to the floor.

There were four of us standing there waiting. Finally, the load master asked us what each of us weighed. We told him.

He did his weight calculations and then told us that only three of us could get on the plane. One of us had to stay. I immediately turned around and walked back to the jeep.

The load master hollered after me and asked me why me. I said that I had two months and three weeks left, and I wasn't in that big of a hurry. I said that I would catch the next flight. I could hear him laughing.

When I think back and reflect on how these two field hospitals impacted my life, I view it with mixed emotion.

I feel fortunate that my wounds were minor compared to most other soldiers. Yet I regret not having stayed in these hospitals longer and letting my body completely heal. Had I done that, I might have avoided some of the problems that have plagued me for the rest of my life.

On both occasions when I was strong enough to stand without getting dizzy or nauseated, I asked to go back to my unit. I argued with the doctors telling them that I was fine when I wasn't. In combat, you get into a rhythm, things that you have to do or don't have to do to stay alive. Anything that disrupts that rhythm makes you nervous and apprehensive. I had the feeling that being in the hospital would cause me to lose my edge. On both occasions when the doctors released me and let me go back to my unit, they gave me pain pills and antibiotics.

When I got back to my unit, I'd wake up in the morning and be in pain. So I would take the pain pills. But shortly thereafter I would start throwing up. After about a week, I figured it out. If I ate something in the morning first and got some food in my stomach, I didn't have a problem holding down the pills. No one told me.

I could not get any water in my ears nor could I even touch the inside of my ears with my fingers or I would get a painful infection. I carried cotton balls with me because if the wind blew, I had to put the cotton in my ears or I would get an infection. It was like that for a couple of years.

The pain in my neck and shoulder was sharp, but the pain pills dulled it. I could deal with it. I learned to block the pain out. But the migraines were brutal. There was no blocking them out.

When I ran out of pain pills, I would go to the medics and get more. The pain pills they had me on were called the thirty percent Darvon. After, the second wounds they put me on was fifty percent Darvon. I could tell the difference. The fifty percent were stronger.

I remember telling a medic that the Darvon was slow working when I first took them. He told me to take them with a beer and they would work faster. He was right. They got me through Vietnam and home.

I remember the first night I got home after completing my one-year tour of duty. My mom, my dad, and I were sitting in the living room talking, and I started to get a migraine. I got up and went to my duffle bag and got out a bottle of Darvon. I took three. I went out to the kitchen and got a cold beer and swallowed the Darvon with the beer.

My mom freaked out. She had worked in a doctor's office. I was naive. I didn't even know that what I was doing was bad.

My mother worked for Dr. Schnoeblen in my home town. Dr. Schnoeblen was well thought of and greatly respected in that part of Kansas. The next day, she had me in his office. She told him what she saw me do.

He asked me why, and I told him. He shook his head, and then he told me to go home and get all of the Darvon and come back. I did. He took the bottle of pills and dumped them down the drain.

He explained that what I was doing was wrong, and he explained to me why. I really didn't know that I was addicted to pain killers. But after his explanation, for the first time, I realized that I was. Up until then, "addicted" meant someone faraway in a big city or Edgar Allen Poe.

He told me that the only way he could help me was for me to be clearheaded and describe my pain to him. I never took another Darvon, but it wasn't easy.

During those thirty days, Dr. Schnoeblen helped me to mentally and physically deal with my wounds. I realize how fortunate I was to have Dr. Schnoeblen.

The migraines stopped several years after Vietnam. But to this day, I can't turn my head more than four inches to the left before pain starts and my ears still ring. I have learned to live with the pain. Now it reminds me of how fortunate I was.

Chapter 6

When I was released from the 93rd Evacuation Hospital, I was reassigned from A Company 1st and the 12th First Cavalry Division to Headquarters Company 2nd and 34th Armored Battalion. I was reassigned because of my contract with the Army. The draft was in effect during the Vietnam War. Draftees had a two-year military obligation. I enlisted for Armor. But because I enlisted, my military obligation was three years. For that additional year, a soldier could choose which combat arms in which he wanted to be trained and serve. I chose Armor, which means tanks. When the army sent me to A Company 1st Cavalry and then sent me to an infantry outfit, this breached my contract.

One of the three soldiers who was sent to the 1st Cavalry with me had also enlisted in Armor. He wrote a letter to his congressman and complained that the Army had breached its contract with him. The congressman in turn contacted the secretary of the Army to make the soldier's case. The secretary agreed with the congressman, and so all three of us were reassigned to the Armored Battalion.

The 2nd and 34th Armored Battalion had both M48 tanks and recon tracks. The official military terminology for the recon track was armored personnel carrier (APC). They have a four-man crew, a track commander (TC), left and right gunners, and a driver. It had 3 machine guns, 2 50 caliber, and 1 M60, 7.62 caliber. We carried a basic load of ten thousand rounds of ammo for the machine guns. We carried a couple of cases of grenades, and the driver on our track had an M79 grenade launcher. Referred to as a forty mike-mike, it took forty millimeter rounds. We also had M16s in case our machine guns jammed.

THE SHADOW OF DEATH

The APC was designed to carry ten soldiers to the battle field along with the four-man crew. We never accomplished that purpose. The APC was about half the size of a tank. It moved much faster, was more maneuverable, and could literally turn 360 degrees on a dime. The APC crew also had a much better view of the battlefield. These were the benefits.

The negatives were that it was much lighter and made of homogenized aluminum. It didn't get stuck as easily as a tank, but the fifty caliber machine gun would go right through an APC and tear the crew apart.

The scariest think about the APC was the 113 model had a V8 gas engine. The NVA found the locations of the gas tanks. They would shoot their rocket-propelled grenades (RPGs) into them which would ignite the fuel tank. An APC fuel tank had a one hundred-gallon capacity, and one gallon of fuel has an explosive capacity of five sticks of dynamite. So when a fuel tank was hit, the track was blown apart, and the crew was incinerated.

Finally, because of the high casualty rate, the gas 113 APC was replaced with the 114, which had a diesel powered engine. Diesel doesn't explode or catch fire. The day the platoon got the replacement track was a day of celebration.

The base camp for the 2nd and 34th was in Long Binh. Long Binh was a small village in the country outside of Saigon. I was told that our battalion was to provide security and intelligence about enemy activity in the Saigon area.

The base camp resembled the base camp of the 1st Calvary, but it was a much smaller version. The outside perimeter was composed of an eight-foot-tall barbed wire fence. Outside the fence were rows of concertina wire with claymore mines between them from the fence out three hundred yards. All vegetation and trees cut down and cleared out down to the ground all the way around the base camp. This area is called the kill zone because the enemy would have to cross three hundred of yards of open ground to attack us. Then he would have to get through rows of barbed wire, concertina wire, and claymore mines before he would get to our fence.

On the inside of the fences, there was a bunker made of sandbags every fifty yards. Each bunker had two soldiers and a machine gun inside. Bunkers went all the way around our perimeter, and they were manned twenty-four hours a day. The main gate entrance had two bunkers, one each on either end of the gate. Soldiers were on duty there twenty-four hours a day. Each of those bunkers had two machines in it.

Our tank companies had seventeen tanks each. Our recon platoon consisted of twelve tracks. Every morning after chow, one of our tank companies and our recon platoon rolled out of our front gate to spend the day looking for the enemy. We rarely found them.

I didn't realize it at the time, but the month and a half spent in the base camp gave me time to learn my track—a Romeo 35—inside and out. I also learned armor tactics, which would be crucial later. We never really engaged the enemy during that time. It was hit and run. The NVA knew we had superior firepower, and they wanted no part of us.

Every morning when we rolled out of the gate, there were a little boy and a little girl standing alongside the road watching us, the same two children every day. He was a couple of years older than the girl. I would have guessed them to be five and three years old. He was always holding her hand, and he always had a serious scowl on his face. I would smile at him as we passed by, but he never smiled back.

Finally, one morning, I had my driver stop the track and I dismounted. I walked over to them and gave them my breakfast fruit, which I had saved. It was an apple, banana, and an orange. I smiled at him and then gave him the fruit. From that day on, every day when I went through the gate, I would stop and give him fruit. When I came back in the afternoon, I would give him two boxes of c-rations, about two meals.

I learned from the village chief that they were orphans. I also would give him peasters, the Vietnamese money. I cared about them. I wanted them to know that there was another side to American soldiers. The scowl turned into a smile, and it gave me something to look forward to each day for the seven weeks that I was there.

I still have a picture of that boy and his little sister.

Some thirty-four years later, the corporation I worked for sent me to San Pablo, California. An investment group of Vietnamese businessmen had bought a mall there. We had a contract with them to be part of the grand opening of the mall. I met with three young Vietnamese men who were in charge of the project. In our first meeting, I was impressed with their education and professionalism. We talked for a length of time over the course of one year, and I got to know them. One day, I met one-on-one with the man in charge of the project. He told me at the conclusion of the project that he was leaving to go to Washington. He belonged to the Young Republican Party, and he had been asked by the president to come to Washington and help with his re-election campaign. We talked about the business at hand, and then our conversation drifted into personal territory. I told him that I had spent a year in Vietnam as an American soldier. He told me that he was a Vietnamese refugee. I told him my story of the little boy and girl. He looked me in the eyes.

"Kurt, I was that little boy."

Chapter 7

Up until now, we had chased the enemy. The NVA ran, and we followed and engaged. They wouldn't stop and fight. They would ambush us and run. Your first time in combat is an experience indelibly etched upon your memory. No one knows for sure how he will react when bullets start flying past his body, or when his first friend is wounded or killed, or when he sees blood and guts for the first time. I believe that courage or cowardice is something you are born with. I've seen a small slight-of-build soldier who might have weighed 140 pounds did an unbelievably courageous thing, and I've seen a 200-pound soldier curled up in a fetal position and cried like a baby from the impact of battle. Fear is something every soldier has in common—fear of never seeing your loved ones again or fear of death.

Fear can be controlled.

This time, we had the enemy trapped in a rectangle of jungle. Three sides of the rectangle were surrounded by open rice paddy fields. If the enemy tried to escape across the open rice paddies, they would be knee-deep in water. They knew that we would call in gunships and helicopters and they would be mowed down and slaughtered. The fourth side was where we began our engagement. We were in a line formation that ran all the way across the open end of the rectangle. The front line consisted of tanks, and in between the tanks were our recon tracks. Some thirty yards behind the line of tanks and recon tracks was a second line composed of infantry.

Air strikes and artillery barrages had been concentrated on the rectangle. They went on for a couple of hours. This is an anxious time because you know that when they stop, you are next. Everything stopped, and it became eerily quiet. The word came over the radio to "move out." A million thoughts raced through my mind. It's an adrenalin rush. It's game time.

You focus on what's ahead of you. You look for movement, a flash of weapon, or the face of the enemy. The noise from the tanks and recon tracks takes away your sound sense. Your eyes are your best friend. I heard a faint buzzing noise started, and I didn't realize what it was until a bullet hit my gun shield six inches in front of me on my fifty-caliber machine gun. That was death, and it was very close. It shook me. I had to reach down inside and grab some guts. Reality had set in. I blocked out the noise and focused on what was in front of me. When you see the first flash from a rifle or a tracer from a machine gun, reflexes and training take over. You return fire. You do everything you can to stay alive.

I was the TC on my track. I sat behind a fifty-caliber machine gun with a steel-plated gun shield in front of me. The gun shield does not protect your head and upper chest. On a fifty caliber, every fifth round is a tracer. Because a machine gun fires so fast, it looked like a stream of fire coming out of the machine gun. You walk tracers into the target. Anything that moves, you shoot.

As we made our push, the further we got into the rectangle, the tougher it got. The NVA dug spider holes. As you moved forward, you had to watch them. You would drop a grenade in the hole. If you didn't, the NVA would let you drive over them, then come up behind you, and shoot you and your crew in the back. The heat was unbearable. It was over a hundred degrees. My eyes were burning. But I was doing okay. I blocked out the bullet sounds and focused on what was in front of me and watched the ground for spider holes. At some point, it became very hard to see. The dust from the tanks and recon tracks, the gun powder from the main guns on the tanks, the machine guns and rifle bullets tearing off pieces of everything they hit and throwing it up in the air put a lot of smoke and debris into my line of sight. The fighting lines became closer. We moved forward slower and slower. Occasionally, I would hear a scream and, every now and then, an NVA trumpet.

I carried a basic load of ten thousand rounds and fifty grenades on my track. I didn't know how long we had been fighting, but I was low on ammo and grenades. The word came over the radio for us to stop. The infantry had to hold the enemy while we went back to a staging area for fuel and ammo. The tanks and recon tracks turned around and went a quarter of a mile to our rear where the staging area had been set up. Helicopters were bringing in diesel fuel, bullets, grenades, water, and hot food. I had a four-man crew, one of which was a medic, and me. I rotated them around. I had one eating, one cleaning machine guns, and one getting ammo and grenades. I went to see my platoon leader to see how we were doing. When all the tanks and recon tracks were resupplied and ready to go, we lined up and waited for the word to move out.

Tanks and recon tracks against straight infantry should be an easy fight, but it wasn't. The NVA fought gallantly. The tanks were M48A3s, which were the medium tanks most commonly used in Vietnam. The main gun was about 90MM, which means the round was about three feet tall and six inches in diameter. The tanks carried three types of rounds. First was a canister. It consisted of ball bearings half the size of marbles. In thick jungle, a tank could fire one round of canister, and it would clear a path thirty feet wide and fifty feet long. The second type of round was flechette. It consisted of hundreds of small steel arrows. The last was white phosphorous. These rounds shot through the trees and would break up in small pieces and fall to the ground. When it fell on a soldier, it would burn right through his flesh. The only way to stop it was to cut it out with a knife immediately. The bad thing about white phosphorous was if the enemy shot a round into the turret on the tank, it would set the phosphorous off inside the turret. It was a horrible way for the tank crew to die. We had only one tank commander who had the courage to carry it on his tank. He was a Mexican staff sergeant with big balls. All the other tank commanders refused to carry phosphorous on their tanks. All of these rounds were devastating on infantry; in addition to that, a tank had two machine guns. The tank commander had a fifty-caliber machine gun mounted next to the main gun.

On each recon track, we had three machine guns. The TC had a fifty caliber, and the right and left gunner had smaller caliber machine guns called M60s. We had a superior firepower, but the NVA were well trained and mentally and physically tough. They would not surrender.

During the next twenty-four hours, I had two more emergency resupplies on ammo and grenades. To stay alive, you had to be good with the fifty. I'd see a puff of smoke or a tracer, and I would swing right into the target. My first few tracers would be very close.

I couldn't remember the last time I had slept. I was soaked in sweat. My eyes were burning. My ears were ringing. I was dirty, tired, and worn out. I was having a tough time seeing because there was so much dust and debris in the air. The going was brutal. We were taking heavy casualties, so we were told to stop again and return to the staging area. The word was that air strikes and heavy artillery would be called in again to soften up the NVA. This time, we all pulled out tanks, recon tanks, and infantry. We went back to the staging area and repeated the same process. We fueled up the tracks, resupplied ammo and grenades, cleaned weapons, ate, and tried to get a few minutes of sleep before we moved out again.

B52s dropped blockbuster bombs on the rectangle, which made huge holes in the ground and caused ear drums to explode. After that, a couple of helicopters flew over the rectangle dropping "Choy Hoy" pamphlets—pieces of paper stating that if you surrendered, you would be taken to a POW camp until the war was over. You would be given job training while you were there, so when the war was over, you could be a productive member of your society. We waited an hour to see if any of the NVA would surrender, but no one did.

They decided to drop napalm on the rectangle, which incinerated everything above ground. All of this took time, and we were thankful for it. We were all lined up ready to go back into battle. I dumped a canteen of water on my head and fell asleep behind my machine gun. The word came down to move out. We tried to go back into the rectangle three times, but the ground was so hot from napalm that we couldn't breathe. We had to back out and let the ground cool off. Just before the word came down to move out for the last time, we were lined up, and I looked at the rectangle. It was shocking.

During the B52 strikes, the ground shook violently. Trees, dirt, and water exploded into the air. I was a half mile away in the staging area, and I could see this. During the artillery barrage, the sky above the rectangle was thick with dust and debris. I had never seen a napalm air strike. The rectangle was instantly a red inferno. I viewed all of this with mixed emotions. I felt pain and sorrow for our dead and wounded, but I felt compassion for the enemy because he was experiencing this up close and personal. This had to be a terrible way to die. What had once been a tropical jungle was now black and charred.

We started back to the rectangle, and I believed that no one could have survived, but I was wrong. About halfway in, the enemy came up out of the ground like rats, and they fought until the last man was killed. The napalm made it easier for us because it burned away the vegetation and cover. The enemy could not hide. But it was brutal. The NVA fought and died like mad men. They amassed all their men in one area and tried to overrun us. For a short time, the rockets and bullets going out equaled the rockets and bullets coming in. Our superior firepower finally overwhelmed them, and the battle slowly but finally came to an end.

I don't know how long we continued to pour our firepower into the NVA before we realized no one was firing back. One by one, the tanks, recon tracks, and infantry stopped firing. It became deathly still. We all looked ahead in disbelief with our fingers still on the triggers, but it was over. I sat there on my track behind my machine gun hoping it was over but not believing that it was. Finally, some of the men started dismounting their tanks and tracks to check out the fallen enemy soldiers. I watched for a while, too tired to move and not taking a chance of getting shot by a possum-playing enemy soldier. As I sat there, I checked out my body. I had no wounds. My crew was okay, and outside of my ears ringing and being filthy and hot, I had made it through my first major battle. I looked up to the sky and saw this big beautiful cloud, and I thanked God for being alive.

Finally, I grabbed by rifle and dismounted my track. I walked straight out in front of my track. I had no idea what to expect. Some soldiers out to my left started to make a pile of enemy weapons. I walked over and looked at the weapons. I picked up a couple of AK-47s, and I realized this was what was firing at me. I decided to go back to my track and get my camera. I was going to take some pictures and send them home to my buddies so they could see I was where the action was. I got the camera and walked straight away from my track. Only this time, I walked further, and I began to see dead enemy soldiers.

I had seen dead men before, but these were in grotesque positions, and some of them were really torn up. I walked slowly and stared at the dead. Nothing had prepared me for this. I couldn't believe what I was seeing. I bent down and touched a dead soldier. Reality set in. I got up and looked back at my track and walked further away from it. I walked around the bodies. I stopped at a hedgerow. There was a trench dug in front of it. It was about three feet wide and three feet deep. I looked in. There were bodies everywhere. It was very hot, and I started to feel lightheaded, so I squatted down. This trench was where they made their last stand.

I looked into the trench. The first dead soldier I saw had been hit across the chest with a machine gun. He had been hit in the lungs. As the air escaped from the bullet holes in his lungs, it had made bubbles of blood. The soldier next to him on his right had no body from the waist down. He had an anti-tank rocket in his right hand. He must have gotten out of the trench to fire the rocket at a tank and got hit by a canister round from that tank. The soldier next to him was lying on his side in the bottom of the trench. His right arm and leg were gone, and I could see into his body cavity. I quickly looked away in the opposite direction. In the side of the trench, a soldier had dug a small ledge back into the dirt. He had placed a candle on the ledge. Next to the candle was a worn picture of a man and a woman with two small girls. They were all holding hands and smiling. I knew that was his wife and daughters. Next to this picture was an aluminum canteen. A picture of a dove of peace and sunrays had been scratched into the canteen. I will always believe the soldier had made that ledge his "death shrine."

He knew that he was going to die. The soldier next to this death shrine had been shot in his left eye, and all that was left was a black hole.

I stood up. As I walked back to my track, I took the camera off from my neck. When I got to my track, I threw the camera inside. My head was swimming. I was sweating profusely. I started walking to try and clear my head. Eventually, I walked to the edge of a bomb crater. It was a big hole in the ground, and in the bottom of it was water. I walked to the edge of the water; I knelt and scooped up water with my hands and threw it in my face. As my head began to clear, I saw the water was red. I looked to my left, and three feet away from my hands, a dead NVA soldier was lying upside down with the top part of his head from the eyebrows being gone. His brains and blood were running into the water. His eyes were open, and so was his mouth. Flies were walking in and out of his mouth and across his eyes.

I got up and walked back to my track. I climbed up behind the machine gun. I just sat there. I watched the other soldiers put the enemy weapons in piles. They also put the dead enemy bodies into piles. They picked up pieces of bodies and put them in piles. The soldiers that were doing this were talking. I could hear their voices, but I couldn't understand what they were saying, and I didn't want to know.

The helicopters from headquarters in Saigon began to arrive, carrying brass and photographers from *Stars and Stripes*. They were taking pictures of everything and interviewing some of the soldiers. Some of the senior officers took flags and weapons and put them in their choppers. I found some of this offensive because I felt that they were desecrating the dead NVA soldiers. I never took one trophy from the dead NVA soldiers, rifles, pistols, flags, or anything else.

But most of all, I never took one single picture.

Chapter 8

When you go through basic and advanced training, some of it sticks, and some of it doesn't. If I was given any training on how to deal with snipers, I didn't remember it. The recon platoon's commanding officer was Lieutenant Davis. (We rarely knew anyone's first name. Sometimes, we didn't know a buddy's full name. We just knew their last names and their rank.) Lieutenant Davis was from Savannah, Georgia. The men in the recon platoon respected him and liked him.

Back in the real world, he was an attorney. He was college educated and a southern gentleman in every sense of the word. I swear he looked just like Rhett Butler in *Gone with the Wind*, right down to the mustache. Every day about an hour before sunset, Lieutenant Davis would go into his track and take out a folding lawn chair and mix himself a martini. He kept a cooler of ice on his track. There were a martini glass, vodka, vermouth, and olives in the ice. He told me that he wasn't going to let this place make a barbarian out of him. While he mixed and drank his cocktail, he would talk about things he loved and missed about home in Savannah. He was soft-spoken, but he always got his message across. He never had to repeat himself. He was something special in combat, and everyone knew it.

Whether we were attacking or being attacked, he instinctively knew how to react. We were always one step ahead of the enemy. His grasp of battle tactics was amazing. We got our confidence and swagger from him. Lieutenant Davis had been told that there was enemy activity in and around a rubber plantation. Our recon platoon and one company of tanks were sent to the plantation to check it out. We traveled down Highway 1, nicknamed Thunder Road.

The nickname came from the fact that the NVA would plant mines in the road at night for us to run over the next day. The trip down the highway was one of apprehension. The highway was bordered on both sides by rice paddies. We had two minesweepers out in front of us, so we were moving slowly. You never knew if the minesweepers would miss one, and we would be unlucky enough to hit it. If a tank hit a mine, it would blow the tracks off. The crew would get concussions and earaches, but they would survive.

Recon tracks were another story. They weighed several thousand pounds less than the tanks, and the mines would blow them apart or into the air. The tanks followed the minesweepers. Then came the recon tracks. We were always hoping that if any of the mines were missed by the sweepers, the tanks would set them off before they got us. But it didn't always work that way. Lieutenant Davis was always the lead track for recon. The third track back belonged to a buck sergeant named Robinson. We called him Robbie. He was the only other soldier in our battalion from Kansas, Junction City. He had played college football. When we were in base camp, he and several of the other guys in our platoon and I spent hours playing football to pass the time. Robbie was scared to death of spiders. He was a good guy.

When the mine went off, I felt the explosion before I heard it. Robbie's track was blown into the air. The track did a somersault and landed upside down. When it landed, Robbie was underneath the track. The gun shield on the fifty-caliber machine gun caught him across the legs right above the knees. It chopped off both of his legs. He crawled away from the track. He looked down and saw that his legs were gone. He looked around, and then he turned back and crawled to the track. By then, it was an inferno. He disappeared into the fire. He never uttered a sound. To this day, I don't know if he crawled inside the burning track looking for his crew or if at the instant he saw his legs were gone, he decided that he didn't want to live that way and ended it. All of this happened so fast. I sat there stunned, not wanting to believe my eyes.

The halfway point to the rubber plantation was the Hoc Mau Bridge. We stayed there overnight. The next morning, we were back on Highway 1 rolling toward the plantation. I couldn't get Robbie out of my mind because I couldn't understand what he had done.

The smell of the rice paddies dragged me back to reality. The Vietnamese used human waste to fertilize the rice fields. The waste, the one hundred-degree heat, and the humidity created a smell that permeated the air and your clothes. We stopped for the night about five miles from the rubber plantation. Before we went to sleep, we cleaned rifles and machine guns. We checked ammo, grenades, the engines, and the tracks. When we finished all checks and maintenance, it would get silent on track. This was the quiet time, and the crew knew and respected it. This was the time we wrote letters home. None of us knew what the next day held for us, but you couldn't help but wonder if this was the last letter you'd ever write home. For some, it was.

The next morning, we rolled out early. Everyone was focused and intense. When we got about a quarter of a mile from the rubber trees, we formed a straight line staggering the recon tracks between the tanks. Then we started our move toward the rubber trees. When we were about two hundred yards out, I remember thinking how straight the rows of trees were. But I changed my focus to the base of the trees. I knew this was where the enemy would be hiding. I didn't think that there was enough vegetation to hide them.

Suddenly, weapons opened up on us. We poured machine gun and tank fire into the vegetation at the base of the trees. Our return fire wasn't slowing down the casualties that we were taking. There was no movement, gun smoke, or barrel flashes coming from the base of the trees. Immediately, the radios got busy. Tracks were calling in soldiers getting hit. Lieutenant Davis came over the radio and told everyone to concentrate all of our firepower into the treetops. We had snipers. I brought the barrel up and started walking the tracers into the treetops. When tank rounds hit the treetops, there were explosions of green. The radio was going berserk, calling in men down and wanting a medic.

The driver on my track was an Italian American. He was from the streets of Chicago, the Italian part of town. When he got care packages from home, they reeked of garlic. It was so strong that all of our mail smelled like garlic. He caught the clap four times, and the medicine they were giving him to clear it up was barely working. He was obsessed with the track. He treated it like it was his own personal hot rod. Everything on the track had to work perfectly. The thing I liked most about him was his toughness. He never complained.

I was focused on pouring machine gunfire into the treetops. Out of the corner of my eye, I saw my driver's head jerk. He slid out of sight down inside the driver's compartment. I dropped down inside from behind my machine gun. Down inside, I was about three feet away from him. He had fallen forward up against the front wall of the track. I couldn't see his face, but I could hear a gurgling sound coming from him. The sniper round hit him in the larynx and came out at the base of his neck. The hole in the back of his neck was too big for him to live. I grabbed him and laid him down. His body was jerking, and blood was pouring out of his mouth. He was in shock and slowly dying.

Alphabet, the medic on my track, and I moved him to the back of the track. Alphabet tried to help him, but all he could do was hold his hand and talk to him until he was dead. I went back up front and tried to get through to Lieutenant Davis on the radio, but it was too busy. I went back to Alphabet, but I could tell by the look in his eyes that my driver was dead.

I told Alphabet that he was going to have to drive. I told him that he had to keep his head down inside the track and use the vision blocks. The vision blocks were glass prisms that allowed you to be down inside the tracks. You could look through them and see outside. By doing this, you weren't exposed to rifle fire. You were below the top deck of the track. I could tell by the radio traffic that we had several guys hit and we were still taking casualties. I got back up in the TC cupola and started concentrating our machine gunfire on the treetops. I couldn't have been firing my machine gun more than five minutes. I looked over at Alphabet to check on him. He had stuck his head back through the driver's hatch. I leaned over toward him. I was going to slap him on the helmet and get his attention. But my fingertips were inches from his head when the round hit him. The back of his helmet exploded. The back of his skull and his brains scattered across the top of the track. In an instant, he was gone.

We laid Alphabet next to my driver. I took one of my machine gunners and put him into the driver's compartment to finish the fight. As quickly as it started, it was over. In a period of less than twenty minutes, we had fourteen men shot through the head or neck. I had lost half of my crew. We found parts of three snipers tied in the top of the rubber trees. A couple of hours later, we put my two men in body bags and loaded them in a chopper. They were going home.

In some ways, I envied them.

<<Insert image: Evacuating wounded from NVA ambush, Filhol rubber plantation>>

Chapter 9

Replacement soldiers who come into a combat unit are referred to as fresh meat. They replace the dead, the wounded, and the soldiers who have completed their one-year tour of duty and were going home. The quality of training they had received would have a lot to do with how well they would survive in combat. Every replacement is given a lot of advice. Some of it is valuable, and some of it is just plain old bullshit. You don't know until you get into combat just how much of this information is relevant or useful. But when you are told one thing over and over again, you realize that this must be important. The advice I got repeatedly was: "Save your last bullet for yourself," and "Don't let the NVA take you prisoner." The reasoning behind that advice hit home a short time later.

I can't remember how long I was in the 2nd and 34th nor how many search-and-destroy mission I'd been on when the following event took place. I can remember in detail what happened. We were in a straight line formation, and we had been pushing through thick elephant grass and brush all day. It was about two hours before dark when we walked into an ambush. We were taking heavy machine gunfire, along with intense small arms fire and RPGs. The track to my immediate left took a hit from an RPG. When Romeo 34 took the hit, it shuddered to a stop and started smoking heavily. The enemy fire we were receiving was so intense that I didn't hear the Romeo 34 TC on the radio until after he took the hit from the RPG, which was a bad sign.

When I finally heard him after several minutes, the commander of Romeo 34 said the RPG didn't hit them head on, which was lucky. It came across the top deck of the track and hit the gun shield of his right side machine gunner. The machine gunner was dead, and the "Kit Carson" that was behind him was wounded and disoriented. He jumped off the front of the track and ran into the line of fire. The TC of Romeo 34 also said his driver was okay as was his left side machine gunner. He said that they had momentarily been stunned by the explosion from the RPG. He also said that he had received some shrapnel but that he was okay and they were once again returning fire.

A "Kit Carson" was the nickname American soldiers used for South Vietnamese soldiers. They were on our side. We used them to go down into the tunnel complexes we found. The Kit Carsons were much smaller than the American soldiers. Their job was dangerous because the tunnels were booby trapped with explosives, venomous snakes, and punji stake pits. Those pits were holes studded with pointed stakes. The stakes were covered with human feces and hidden with grass. If the stake didn't kill, the feces would cause serious, sometimes fatal, infections to those who were unfortunate enough to fall in. I don't know what the life expectancy for a Kit Carson was, but it couldn't have been long because we never had the same one twice.

We found out later that when the RPG hit Romeo 34's gun shield, part of the shrapnel hit the Kit Carson and the explosion disoriented him. He jumped off the track wounded and stunned. Instead of retreating to the rear behind the track, he ran straight into the enemy fire with no weapon to defend himself. How far he made it into the enemy field of fire before he was cut down, we couldn't tell because of the tall elephant grass and brush, but we could hear him screaming for help.

A soldier named Stanley from another track dismounted and headed toward Kit Carson on foot to help him. Stanley was a country boy from someplace down south. He had jet-black hair and a real fair complexion. Stanley couldn't tan, and the Vietnam sun turned his skin red. He looked like a lobster. Twice he got close enough to see Kit Carson. Both times, he was knocked down by bullets. His flak jacket kept the bullets from penetrating into his body. I spent one year in combat, and this was the only time I ever saw a flak jacket protected a soldier like Stanley's did that day. After he was knocked down the second time, he retreated back to his track. He had been unsuccessful. Shortly thereafter, we were given the order to back out of the firefight. By then it was almost dark; we retreated to an assembly area close by for the night.

We could hear Kit Carson's screams. They continued most of the night. They were agonizing. None of us slept that night. We asked our ranking officer many times if we could try to bring him back. We were told no because the NVA were waiting for us and that was what they wanted us to do. We knew the officer was right, but it was hard to listen to the screams, knowing that we were his only hope.

About an hour before daylight, the screams stopped. At daylight, air strikes saturated the area where we had been ambushed. Finally, a couple of hours later, we were given the order to return to the area where we had been ambushed. This time, we received no enemy fire, not one shot. We moved through the area slowly and carefully. Finally, we found what was left of the Kit Carson. The NVA had crucified him, skinned him, and cut off his genitals. At first, I couldn't believe what I was seeing. No sane person could do this to another human. It was way beyond brutality.

We all looked in disbelief at what we were seeing. But if the NVA's purpose was to frighten us, it failed. We felt contempt and a burning hatred for the NVA. If it accomplished anything, it strengthened our resolve to punish the enemy at every opportunity. We would not forget what we saw that day and what the NVA had done to Kit Carson.

Chapter 10

Every combat unit in war has a reputation—some good, some bad, most average, but only a few exceptional.

The 2nd and 34th was one of only two armor battalions in Vietnam. It was a "special" battalion. When it was formed in the States, it was formed to be "special." All of its officers and senior NCOs were from West Point, the Army's War College. They were the best of the best. The battalion's commander was Colonel Staylee, also known as Warrior Six. He was an exceptional officer in every way and proved that with the 2nd and 34th. To the best of my knowledge, no other battalion in Vietnam had all West Pointers as staff and chain of command.

<<Insert image: The 2nd and 34th on the move to relieve embattled troops at "the Battle of Suoi Tre," War Zone C, Republic of Vietnam>>

By the time the 2nd and 34th Armored engaged the enemy in the Battle of Suoi Tre/LZ Gold (as it is known in the annals of the Vietnam conflict), it was combat experienced. The Battle of LZ Gold was one of only a few major battles that the American forces won a decisive victory over the NVA. Sometime after the battle, General William Westmoreland, commander of the American forces in Vietnam, presented the 2nd and 34th with a Presidential Citation. General Westmoreland told us that the Presidential Citation was for the largest body count in a one-day battle against the enemy and that the 2nd and 34th had distinguished themselves and the United States Army. General Westmoreland then decorated some of our soldiers and our battalion commander, Colonel Staylee. The colonel received a Silver Star for valor.

A large number of top brass flew in from headquarters in Saigon. They brought the news media with them including the *Stars and Stripes*, the military newspaper. The *Stars and Stripes* played the battle as a huge victory for the Americans. I still have a picture that a photographer for the paper gave me that day of the general's visit and ceremony. The battalion was told that there were more than 1,200 dead enemy soldiers on the battlefield, and we found nearly 600 dead that the retreating NVA dragged off with them into the jungle.

LZ Gold was a newly established base camp just inside the "iron triangle." This name came from the fact that this triangle of land was surrounded by the Saigon River on the west and the Tinh River on the east. The "iron" part of the nickname was because this triangle was known to be an NVA stronghold. The artillery unit was there to fire artillery support missions for any American units working in that area. The infantry was there to protect the artillery unit and secure the base camp. LZ Gold was an outpost consisting of one company of infantry, roughly one hundred soldiers, and one battery of artillery about the same size. I don't know what Army unit the infantry was, but I do remember that the artillery unit was the 5th and the 2nd. They were nicknamed the nickel deuce.

LZ Gold hadn't been there long. The company had established a circle perimeter. The infantry had put out rows of barbed wire and claymore mines. They had started clearing all of the vegetation down to the dirt, out and away from the outside of the circle to form a kill zone. They had been working on this daily. The enemy had to cross open ground before he got to our perimeter. The wider the kill zone, the better chance you had of defending your position.

The infantry had about a 150-yard wide kill zone. Inside the perimeter, they had built bunkers with machine guns in them, all around. Between the bunkers, there were 105 howitzer artillery pieces. Militarily speaking, they had a defendable position.

The 2nd and 34th had been moving for days toward LZ Gold. The NVA knew that the battalion was on its way to reinforce it. The officer in charge of it made the mistake of sending his recon team out every morning at the same time and bringing them back every afternoon at the same time. The NVA was watching, and they learned the unit's timing. Then they planned their attack around that schedule.

When the recon team went out that morning, the NVA was in the jungle waiting to kill them.

Once the recon team was dead, the NVA put on the team's fatigues and headed back toward the perimeter. There was a reinforced regiment of about three thousand NVA in the jungle. They had surrounded LZ Gold. The Vietnamese soldiers in American uniforms went to the gate at the perimeter and opened up on the GIs with rifles. This was the signal for the mass ground attack to start. By the time the Army soldiers at the gate realized that this wasn't their recon team, it was too late. I don't believe that the LZ Gold recon team could have been too good to not know that the NVA were in the immediate area, but they didn't.

The battalion commander, Colonel Staylee, got the call from the artillery commander telling him if he didn't get there in the next fifteen minutes, they all would be dead and that the artillery commander and the LZ were being overwhelmed by the NVA. The enemy knew that the 2nd and 34th were close, but they believed that the battalion had no way to get across the river with our tanks and recon tracks. The NVA had not seen tanks, nor had they fought an armor battalion before. The battalion had three armored vehicle launched bridges (AVLBs) with them. AVLBs were portable extendable bridges. The river hardly slowed the 2nd and 34th movement at all. When Colonel Staylee got the call from the artillery commander at the LZ, the battalion had already crossed the river and was about ten minutes away. Colonel Staylee was above the battalion in a Huey helicopter leading the attack.

The battalion had A, B, and C companies with them. Each one of these companies had seventeen M48A1 tanks and the headquarters recon platoon with ten APC, each with three machines guns. Each tank had two machine guns and the main gun.

Just before the battalion broke through the jungle, with Colonel Staylee above and out in front, the battalion started the attack. Colonel Staylee had the chopper pilot fly him to the gate in the perimeter.

This is where the attack started, and the NVA in American uniforms had taken control of one of the 105 howitzers. The NVA were firing it back into the American soldiers. Colonel Staylee jumped out of the helicopter and shot the three NVA on the howitzer with his pistol. Then he got back into the chopper and coordinated the attack.

That was the most courageous act by an officer of the battalion that I had ever seen. It earned him the Silver Star for valor.

When the battalion broke through the jungle in a line formation, we moved slowly through the kill zone. The American's firepower shocked them. They didn't know what to do. The main guns on the tanks were firing canister rounds. They were like giant shotguns. A tank would fire, and there would be an explosion of blood, arms, legs, and body parts flying through the air. The NVA wouldn't retreat, and they were being brutally slaughtered. For the battalion, it was payback for the ambushes, being outnumbered by them and, most of all, for their cruelty to our wounded and captured.

The NVA tried en masse to get up on top of the tanks, which they accomplished, but their rifles and grenades were useless against the thick steel skin on the tanks. All they accomplished was to chip the tanks' paint jobs. Finally, the tanks would have to shoot at each other with the canister rounds to knock the NVA off. The tank commanders could be heard on the radio saying, "Scratch my back," which meant shoot a load of canister at me and blow the NVA soldiers off the turret and the back deck.

The back deck of a tank was composed of heavy steel grates. Below them was the drive system for the tank, which consisted of a diesel engine, a huge transmission, and rear end. At the bottom of the engine compartment were six-inch portholes that drained water out of the engine, transmission, and rear end when they were pressure washed. When the tanks first started shooting at each other to get the NVA soldiers off the turret and the back decks, the soldiers in the recon platoon were behind them and could see red fluid pouring out of the potholes on the tanks. We realized that it was blood from the NVA soldiers, who were being blown off the tanks.

When the battalion broke through the jungle, the tanks were in a line formation. One end of the line was up against the barbed wire perimeter of the LZ Gold compound. The rest of the line stretched across the kill zone to the jungle. The line of tanks were peeling the NVA off the perimeter wire while the battalion slaughtered the NVA as they slowly moved through the kill zone.

The recon tracks were some fifty yards behind the tanks. The line of tanks kept as close together as they could, but they needed thirty-yard gaps between tanks to be able to move their turrets. The tracks, too, kept as close together as we could, and we interlocked our machine gunfire. Some of the NVA poured through the gaps between the tanks at us. We were waiting for them. Each track had three machine guns, which meant with our fourteen tracks, we had forty-two machine guns. The field fire we poured into the NVA infantry was gruesome. The dead and dying were everywhere. The battle seemed to last forever. Finally, what was left of the NVA broke off the attack and headed back into the jungle. Once they retreated, Colonel Staylee called in air strikes on them. Not many of the NVA could have survived. The NVA soldiers had a day from hell, and they deserved it.

The battlefield in front of the tanks was gruesome. There were arms, legs, hunks of flesh, and blood everywhere. This battlefield was full of dead enemy soldiers, and this just as easily could have been the company of infantry and battery of artillery.

The tanks with bulldozer blades on them had to dig trenches to bury the NVA dead.

The battalion told us that we lost fewer than twenty men that day, but the NVA lost almost two thousand. From that day forward, everyone involved in the Vietnam War knew who the 2nd and the 34th were, including the enemy. "Hanoi Hannah," the Vietnamese radio personality who made English-language broadcasts for the North Vietnamese directed at American troops, came over their propaganda radio station announcing there was a $2,000 bounty on every soldier in the 2nd and 34th. She talked about the battalion a lot and said that the NVA would wipe us out. The battalion members felt no compassion then or now for the enemy because they would have slaughtered all of the infantry and artillery soldiers at LZ Gold.

<<Insert image: General Westmoreland addresses members of the 2/34>>

Chapter 11

I sustained injuries and was transported by medevac twice, but none of my injuries were life-threatening. I saw many wounded men. Some of the seriously wounded would look at their wounds and see the destruction and blood. You would see the fear in their eyes. They thought they were going to die, so they would give up, go into shock, and slip away. Others had made up their minds that they would not die in this place. I came to believe that genetics, mental toughness, and the will to live determined survival.

We had an eighteen-year-old soldier by the name of Cotillion Cross in my company. We called him C.C. He was Black and from the rural Mississippi Delta. He was a good soldier, and I liked him. He was raised poor and was humble, but he had dignity. He would tell us stories about his life in the Delta and had a way of putting a humorous spin on everything, good or bad.

C.C. was a driver on a tank. These tanks had a four-man crew—commander, gunner, loader, and driver. The driver sat below the floor of the turret, down in a small compartment. The compartment was out front and dead center in the tank.

During training, troops learn that the skin on the tank is a foot thick at its thinnest point. The only things the NVA had that would damage a tank were explosive mines and RPGs. The RPG was an armor-piercing heat round. It was an antitank rocket. It looked like a spear with a broom handle on it. The mechanism the NVA used to fire them looked cheap and phony, but they were deadly. The firing mechanism consisted of a piece of bamboo about three feet long that had been cut in half. The trigger assembly looked like that of a cap pistol that we used to buy at the five- and ten-cent store for a dollar.

The first time I saw an RPG, it was from some dead NVA that we captured after a battle. Just looking at one, it didn't look like it could be as destructive as it was, but they struck fear in us.

The RPGs were twos, sevens, or elevens. The rocket would hit the tank, heat up the metal at the point of impact, and then explode. All of this happened in a millisecond. The RPG twos weren't powerful enough to go in one side of a tank and out the other. Instead, they would go in one side and fly around the inside of the tank. When the RPG hit the tank, it turned the red hot metal into shrapnel which was devastating to the crew. It set off the ammo in the turret, which turned the tank into an inferno. The RPG sevens and elevens were powerful enough to go all the way through the tank. If you weren't between where it went in and where it came out, you had a good chance of surviving. You would have shrapnel and burn wounds, but you would make it.

Otherwise, it was a deadly weapon.

The NVA soldier using the RPG had to be within fifty yards of the tank to be effectively accurate. The NVA would dig a small hole or trench. They would lie down, then pop up and fire the rocket, and then drop back down. It happened so quickly that it was hard to knock them down before they fired. Yet if you didn't, the consequences were devastating. We hung sandbags on the outside of the tanks and recon tracks to pre-detonate the RPGs. It helped.

We were on a search-and-destroy operation. We were in a line: tank, recon track, and tank. We were spaced out and moving through heavy brush. Suddenly, all hell broke loose. C.C. was driving the tank to my left, and it took three direct hits from the RPGs. A tank weighs fifty-two tons, and it still shuddered from the impact of the rockets. It rolled to a stop, and smoke started pouring out of the tank commander's hatch. I tried to raise them on the radio but nothing. I stopped my track. I put one of my crew in the TC copula behind my machine gun. I went out the back of my track and ran to the back of the wounded tank. I climbed up the back side of the turret and looked inside the hull; I couldn't see very well because of the smoke. I called out to see if anyone was still alive. No one answered. I didn't want to climb down inside the turret. I knew it could blow any second. I looked for flames or anything that would give me a good reason not to climb down inside the turret. There weren't any, so I went in feet first.

It was about a seven-foot drop to the floor. There was so much blood on the floor that I slipped and I fell down immediately. The TC, the loader, and the gunner were dead. Hunks of flesh had been ripped from the bodies of the TC and the gunner. I touched them and shook them, but there wasn't a breath left in either one of them. The loader was lying face down in a pool of his blood. Half of his neck was gone. I looked away from him and crawled over to the driver's compartment. I came up behind him. I heard him moan.

I pulled on the back of the seat and C.C. turned his head. I asked him if he was hit, but he didn't respond. The back of the driver's seat was on a pipe that I lifted up and out of the way. I was talking, but he wasn't answering. I put my chin on his shoulder and put my hands under his arms and locked them together across his stomach. I started to pull on him, and my hands got all wet and slick. I leaned my head further forward and looked at his stomach. The muscle that kept his insides in was blown away. His guts fell into my hands. At the same time, I got a smell of his insides. The smell hit me so hard that I got light headed. It was like the smell you get when you gut a deer and open up the body cavity. I leaned back away from him to get away from the smell.

My head began to clear.

I took my shirt off and laid it across his stomach. I tied the arms of the shirt around his waist. I took off my pistol belt and tied it around the other end of the shirt and around his chest. I grabbed him under his arms and pulled him up out of the driver's compartment. I didn't know how I was going to get him through the top hatch of the turret. He was moaning and fading in and out of consciousness. I was frantic. I thought that the tank was going to blow any second. The blood and gore around me made it nearly impossible to stand up, and I had a wounded soldier who couldn't help me.

I looked back up at the hatch at the top of the turret, and there was a face looking back at me. It was the medic off my track. I picked C.C. up and lifted him high enough where the medic could grab his arms. The medic leaned down through the hatch, and I slowly lifted him up. I was afraid that C.C.'s insides would fall down on top of me, but we finally got him up through the hatch. I was covered in C.C.'s blood. It was in my eyes and my mouth. I climbed up through the turret. We took him down the backside of the turret, over the engine compartment, and onto a track fender. Then the medic and I jumped to the ground. We slid C.C. off the tank and carried him back to a bomb crater.

The medic started working on him while I called in a medevac chopper. We loaded him onto the chopper. I didn't believe he had a chance of making it, but the chopper pilot told me later that C.C. had been alive when they arrived at the hospital.

After I finished my tour of duty in Vietnam, I was sent to Fort Hood, Texas, to finish my time in the Army. I had been back in the states about five months. One day when we had finished noon chow at the mess hall and roll call, I started to go to the arms room when I saw this skinny black soldier walking toward me. Once he came closer, I could see tears in his eyes. I didn't recognize him at first, but when he said, "It's C.C.," I knew.

He must have had that special will to live, but I couldn't believe that he made it. He put his arms around me and cried. I was shocked to hear that he remembered quite a bit of what had happened to him. He remembered lying on the operating table, and the doctor was holding his intestines up to the light looking for holes from shrapnel. He had been through several skin grafts that he needed to cover the area of his abdomen that had been blown away. But the best news was that as soon as he got his medical release, he was headed home to the Delta.

<<Insert image: This is one of our tanks that hit a mine up at Wuc Pho. The rounds are going off in the tank>>

Chapter 12

Our battalion had been on a search-and-destroy mission near the Cambodian border. We didn't know it at the time, but our objective was to take the fort at Katum. The French built Katum during their war with the NVA. It was an isolated outpost in the middle of the jungle. The French had learned quickly how hard it was to defend.

We had encountered only minor firefights on our way to Katum. They were tactical maneuvers by the NVA to slow us down and for them to better prepare for their defense of the fort. When we got there, we battled the NVA; and after two days of heavy fighting, they retreated and abandoned the fort to us. Believing they would counterattack us with reinforcements from Cambodia, we dug in and prepared for what was coming.

The first night that we were there, I was told to take a three-man team off my track and put a fifty-caliber machine gun on top of the abandoned NVA bunker next to my track. The French had built bunkers at one hundred-yard intervals all along the outside perimeter of the fort. The bunkers were about four feet underground and about three feet aboveground. The aboveground portion of the bunker had a steel frame with sheets of corrugated metal covered with sandbags. The bunkers were built well and looked solid, but what we couldn't see was that they were infested with rats, insects, and snakes in the ceilings, walls, and floors.

About an hour before dark, rifle fire and screams erupted from the bunker next to us. A soldier in the bunker shot and killed a king cobra.

Shortly after that, one of my crew was stung by a scorpion. The sting wasn't life-threatening, but it was painful and it made him very sick.

We sat the fifty-caliber machine gun on top of a tripod on the roof on the bunker. I had my men get cans of ammo and place them next to the fifty. Then I cleaned and timed it. We thought that we were ready.

Next to the bunker, there was a large pile of trash. It consisted mostly of discarded food and human waste from the NVA soldiers that had manned these bunkers before we arrived. I could see rats and snakes moving around in the trash pile. The pile stunk, but the rats and snakes didn't bother me. I had told my machine gun team that we'd have two men on top of the bunker manning the machine gun and one man down inside the bunker sleeping. We would rotate every two hours. Right about dark, the trash pile came alive with rats. We had a full moon which made it easy to see at night. There were so many rats that it actually looked as if the trash pile was moving. It was an eerie sight.

I was the first soldier to go down inside the bunker to sleep.

A military cot had been left behind. I was going to sleep on it. I had no more than laid down on the cot in that the rats started to run. They were running around on the floor. They would get into fights, which didn't bother me. I was a country boy, and I had seen rats before. I ignored them. I heard something and looked up, but I couldn't see anything because it was dark and there were no available lights in the bunker. I knew by the dirt falling on me that the rats were running around on the ceiling.

I got off the cot and went to the track and got a couple of poncho liners, short nylon blankets. I returned to the bunker and laid down on the cot. I took one of the poncho liners and tucked it under the sides of my chest and over my head. It reached only to my waist. I took the second poncho liner and tucked it under my boots and under the side of my legs. I was dead tired and needed to sleep. I still could hear and feel the dirt falling from the rats running around on the ceiling, but I ignored it and started to doze off. The rats crawled up on the cot and started running over my body. I tried to ignore them and did until one of them stopped and started to gnaw on the poncho liner covering my face.

I got up and went on top of the bunker and slept next to a machine gun where the other two soldiers could keep the rats off me for the two hours of sleep. We rotated all night behind and alongside the machine gun, keeping the rats off the sleeping soldier.

The next morning, we found out that four of our soldiers had been bitten by rats during the night. One of the bitten soldiers was a friend of mine. He told me that a rat bit him on the nose and wouldn't let go. He had to get another soldier to help. They killed the rat and then pried its mouth open. The sergeant had to get rabies shots. He told me that the needle they used for the shots looked like it was a foot long and that the shots were given in a circle around the belly button. The shots weren't really that painful, he said, but they itched like crazy. His stomach was raw from scratching.

We stayed at the old French fort waiting for a counterattack that never came. After a week, we abandoned the fort and headed back for Tay Ninh, our base camp. I have wondered, on occasion, if the reason the NVA never counterattacked us was because of our battalion's reputation or because they were more afraid of the rats and snakes that infested the fort. There was always something vile in this country, but I guess that was good because it kept us focused and kept our minds off our families and homes.

<<Insert image: Tank crew fighting army ants and searching for NVA, Filhol rubber plantation>>

Chapter 13

Combat has a way of changing a soldier's priorities. Every combat soldier finds a source of strength. Each soldier draws from this strength during his time of need. It gives him the will to mentally and physically survive. He has something to cling to. With some, it's their grandparents, parents, wives, children, or maybe even another family member or friend. With others, it's spiritual.

I was close to death many times. I could feel it, I could see it, and I could taste it. On two occasions, God intervened and let me know that He had spared my life. For many years, I never talked about the two experiences because I felt like they were between God and myself. Now, I feel it's time, and I need to express my gratitude.

Our beliefs define us.

We had engaged the enemy in a major battle from which they could neither run nor escape. We had been pushing them for four straight days. When the tanks and recon tracks began to run low on fuel, ammo, and grenades, the infantry would hold the battle line while we returned to a resupply area, about four hundred yards behind the battle line. We'd fill up on diesel, rifle and machine gun ammo, and grenades. Then we'd get fresh water and a hot meal, which had been flown in by helicopters. We'd clean all of our weapons, and then we'd line up with all of our tanks and recon tracks and wait for the order to move out and return to the battlefield. While we were in this line sitting on our recon tracks and tanks, we tried to catch a little sleep. Sleep kept our mind off of what we were returning to.

I was sitting in the TC's cupola behind my fifty-caliber machine gun dozing when a first lieutenant named LaRoche came up to my track and hollered at me. He told me that a helicopter had flown all of the battalion's mail in and I needed to go with him and break the mail down by platoon for our company. I told him that we would be moving out at any minute, and I couldn't leave my track. He argued that I had been in the company the longest and was the only one who knew what platoon every soldier was in. I told him that I understood that, but if I left with him, I might not make it back before the move out. I argued that I needed to stay with my men. We argued back and forth, but finally, he gave me a direct order to get down off my track and go with him.

He outranked me. I had to comply.

I put another soldier in charge of my track, and I went with First Lieutenant LaRoche. We walked over to the helicopter and got the bag of mail, and I started breaking it down by platoon.

I had no more than started when the order came down to move out, and my track and crew left without me. I finished breaking down the mail and walked over to a command track. This track was left in the rear to coordinate resupplies to the front line. It had a radio on it, and I could listen to the communications going on between the platoon leaders now in battle with the NVA. I had been listening to the radio for about ten minutes when the recon platoon leader said Romeo 35, my track, had taken a direct hit from an RPG and that the three-man crew were all KIA, killed in action.

I was stunned. I walked away from the radio. I sat down, letting what I had just heard sink in. I don't know how much time passed, but I looked up at the sky. It was a sunny day, and there were big thunderhead clouds. As I looked at the clouds, a sense of peace came over me. I knew I had been spared.

That was the first time.

The second time I was made aware of my life being spared was on my way home. Four other soldiers and I were loaded onto an Air Force C-130 cargo plane and were heading home. I hadn't slept in four days; my mind and body were in a fog. We had left Saigon and were someplace out over the ocean when the Army major sitting next to me began talking to me. He asked where I was from, and I told him. He saw the 1st Calvary patch on the shoulder of my uniform and asked me what unit I was in. I replied, "A Company 1st and the 12th."

He got a quizzical look on his face, and then he asked me when I had reported to my company. He asked if I had worked in staff back at the base camp.

"No," I replied. "I went into combat with my company."

He said that A Company 1st and 12th had gone into the Happy Valley six weeks after I said I'd reported to them and were wiped out. "I know this is true," he said, "because I was in B Company 1st and 12th."

As I began to think about what he was saying, my mind began to clear. I told him again when I arrived at A Company in Ane Khe. I told him four days after arriving at A Company, I was sent into combat with my company. I had been in A Company twenty-eight days when I was wounded and sent to the 93rd Evacuation Hospital by medevac for ten days, and for some unknown reason, I was taken from A Company and reassigned to Headquarters Company recon 2nd and 34th. When I was released from the hospital and given orders, I was flown to Thon Sung Nehuet base camp to Headquarters Company for the 2nd and 34th. As I worked my way through the time frame and the days since I arrived in Vietnam, I finally figured it out. Three days after I arrived at the base camp for the 2nd and 34th, A Company had gone back into the Happy Valley and were overrun and lost all but twelve men in the company.

As the reality of what I had just figured out hit me, it felt like all the air was sucked out of my lungs and I couldn't breathe. Slowly, a sense of peace came over me. I understood. I had been spared. Yet I made no sound. Once again, I knew. I remember the major putting his hand on my shoulder and saying, "Son, it's all right."

And it was.

Chapter 14

Our battalion had a policy of sending all of the combat soldiers back to our base camp out of combat when they had thirty days left in country. It was great for morale to know that our last days would not be spent in harm's way.

We had just come back from Operation Yellowstone on the Cambodian border. Our base camp was about three miles from Nui Bah Den, which meant the Black Virgin Mountain in Vietnamese. The terrain around our camp was flat and consisted of rice paddies and jungle. The mountain was large and the only thing that was scenically impressive in the entire area. Fog and mist covered the mountain in the mornings, but as the sun heated up, it burned off. The North Vietnamese had tunnel complexes in the mountain where they stored their supplies. Periodically, we would travel up the mountain to run the NVA off. It was always a tough battle, as we had to fight while traveling up hill. I would look at the mountain and think of its beauty. Then my thoughts would drift to my friends who had died on there.

Our base camp was an outpost in the middle of NVA and Viet Cong country and was always getting hit with mortars and rockets. Our first day back in base camp after returning from Operation Yellowstone was spent sleeping. We were physically and mentally exhausted.

In the days to follow, you are always pulling maintenance on the track and weapons, training replacements, catching up on letters, and hoping you won't be going back into battle. I had finally made it to the last thirty days. After about six months in combat, your hometown, friends, and family seem like only a dream. Combat is about minute-by-minute survival. We had been back in base camp about ten days. Five of us buck sergeants were in my hooch, which is a tent with a wooden floor and sandbag walls. We were playing poker, drinking beer, and talking about what we were going to do when we got home. We drank and played cards until the wee hours of the morning.

The next day was January 31, 1968, the day the Tet Offensive started. Tet, the lunar New Year, was supposed to be a time of cease fire. Instead, all over North Vietnam, the NVA had made a major push to overrun the Americans. Tay Ninh was being hit real hard, so Warrior 6 sent our recon platoon and a company of tanks down to help them. They were being overwhelmed. The tank company and recon platoon made it to Tay Ninh, turned the tide, and were holding our position. The next day about noon, the officer in charge of the battle called our command center. Everyone in a combat unit had a line number. Mine was 35. If you were a casualty of war, they would say line 35 was WIA (wounded in action) or KIA (killed in action).

I was standing next to our sergeant major at our battalion bunker when the battlefield officer in charge started calling off the line number status of our troops. Four of the soldiers who were killed were the men I was playing cards with just twenty-four hours earlier: Sergeant Jans, Sergeant Lucas, Sergeant Kerns, and one other whose name slips my memory. I got a sick, hollow feeling as I walked out of the command bunker.

The sergeant major came out to the bunker a few minutes later and asked me if I would pack up their personal belongings so that they could be sent back to their families. I walked over to the hooch and one by one got their duffle bags, took their personal belongings out of their foot lockers and wall lockers, and packed it all up. It was touching packing letters from home and family pictures. But it was also heartbreaking. I took their duffle bags over to S-4 to be sent back to their families.

The sergeant major said, "You know we lost half of our recon platoon and all of our experienced squad leaders. I know you have less than thirty days left in country, but I have new replacements coming in this afternoon, and I need someone to take them to Chew Ly."

The next day, the lieutenant and I, along with thirty new troops, and eighteen other soldiers with some experience took a resupply convoy to Tay Ninh. We had semi-tankers full of fuel and five-ton trucks loaded with ammo, grenades, and medical supplies. We also have five recon tracks and two other trucks full of South Vietnamese soldiers. We lined up the convoy. The lieutenant in a jeep with a driver was the lead vehicle. I was fifty yards behind him in the first recon track. I had three machine guns on my track, and my driver had an M79 grenade launcher. We staggered troop trucks and recon tracks between supply trucks and tankers. I was apprehensive. I had five experienced track crews, not nearly enough men, and no air support. The enemy was raising hell everywhere.

Highway 1, nicknamed Thunder Road, ran between our base camp and where we had to go. I was hoping we would pick up another military convoy. We needed the help. If we got an early start, hustled, and had no problems, we could make Tay Ninh before dark. The lieutenant gave the signal, and we started. We had a game plan, but we knew we'd get slaughtered if we got hit hard.

I kept asking myself, "What the hell am I doing here?"

I really felt sorry for the lieutenant. He was fifty yards out ahead of me in a jeep that had no armor and no top. In the back seat, a machine gun was mounted tall enough to shoot over the driver's and passengers' heads. These three were sitting ducks. We rolled nonstop. We were making good time. I thought that we were going to make it to Tay Ninh before dark.

We were about ten miles outside Tay Ninh when we got hit. A machine gun opened up on the lieutenant's jeep from the jungle, two hundred yards off the road to my left. I swung the fifty-caliber machine gun around and started walking the tracers into their machine gun. The lieutenant had turned the jeep around and was hauling ass back toward me. I saw them out of the corner of my eye as they passed me on my right side. The jeep was all shot to hell, but they were all okay. The machine gun had stopped firing, but we were receiving small arms fire from both sides, and they started dropping mortars on us. It was an overcast day with a low ceiling, which is very bad if you need air support. The only help we could get was from the artillery.

When the lieutenant went by me, he gave the circle sign which meant to wagon wheel up. I did a one hundred eighty-degree turn with my track and followed the lieutenant. We were returning fire and trying to get into a defensive position at the same time. There was a flat, solid piece of ground one hundred yards to our rear, just off the road. It was big enough to get the convoy into a wagon wheel. The road we were on was two and one half lanes wide. It dropped off into the rice paddies on both sides, so turning around wasn't easy for the trucks that had the soldiers in them. The tankers couldn't turn around. They had to back up to the wagon wheel area. The lieutenant had turned around, and I had turned around and was following behind him in his tracks. You always stayed in the same tracks to avoid mines. The vehicle behind me had turned around and was in my tracks.

The first five vehicles had turned around, and we were doing okay when the truck load of soldiers backed off the side of the road and hit a mine. I was just going by them when they hit it. It blew the soldiers out of the truck, and some of them flew over the top of my head. The blast from the mine threw me against the opposite side of the machine gun. The right side of my face and arm felt wet. We were all moving fast, and I didn't stop. We needed to get into our defense position as quickly as possible. I reached over and touched my wet face and arm. It was bloody. I didn't feel any pain, but I couldn't hear out of my right ear. I ran my hand down the side of my face and arm trying to find a wound. I looked at my hand again, and it was covered with blood and human tissue.

We finally got positioned and were returning fire. The rice paddies went out about two hundred yards on either side of the road. At the edge of the rice paddies, the jungle started, and this was where the NVA were entrenched. We finally got artillery support. They walked artillery rounds right down the edge of the jungle on both sides of the road, and the gunfire stopped. It gave us a chance to regroup.

About an hour before dark, two Chinook helicopters came in. They brought three 105 howitzer artillery pieces with crew. I walked over to one of the chopper pilots and started talking to him. I told him I had twenty days left in country. He said he knew that and he was supposed to take me out of the area with him. He told me that they were expecting to get overrun, and they brought the howitzers and crews in to give the soldiers a chance. He told me to get my gear; we were leaving.

I went to my track and got my weapon and my ruck sack. I went over to the lieutenant and my men to tell them that I was flying out. They knew that I was "short," and they understood. I started for the chopper, and I heard one of them say, "What are we going to do now?"

"I don't know," I heard the lieutenant reply.

I went to the chopper pilot and said, "I can't leave these guys like this."

"Get in the chopper," he said.

"I can't do that to these guys." I turned and walked back to my track. The men started cheering, and I was wondering if I had just given myself a death sentence.

The first lieutenant and I got all of the men together.

"I don't want to die in this shit hole," I told them. "If you want to live to see tomorrow, you better get tough and you better get focused, and we need to get ready for what is about to come."

We had four men on each track. I had one man clean weapons and another bring ammo and grenades. The third man ate and the next slept. We all rotated. I told them that they would hit us between 2 and 3 a.m. We would be outnumbered, but we had superior firepower, and we had to crisscross our machine gun lanes so that they couldn't get between us. They would blow trumpets and that they would scream when they came at us. When you think they are going to overwhelm you, fight harder. Decide you don't want to die and that you will do whatever it takes to stay alive. I dismissed them, and I went to my track.

I carried a pocket Bible in my left breast pocket for eleven months and ten days. I took it out, and I wrote on the blank first two pages of it. I wrote a note to my mom, dad, and sisters telling them that I loved them and that I was lucky to have the family that I had. I also told them the only regret I had was that I had not left a son behind. I prayed that if I died, my pocket Bible would get back to them.

Then I got ready for the enemy. The enemy never came. One hour after daylight, we moved out. We made it to Chew Ly without a single shot fired at us. I caught a chopper and flew back to our base camp.

Chapter 15

The chopper ride back to our base camp took a couple of hours. I was relieved to be up high enough so that the bullets couldn't touch me, and I could relax for a few minutes. As we flew over the countryside, I thought about how peaceful and harmless it looked. Yet I felt sad for my dead brothers knowing that death lurked everywhere.

When I got back to base camp, the sergeant major assured me that I wouldn't be leaving again until I caught the "Freedom Bird" home. I was down to fifteen days. Every minute seemed like an hour. I would get up, eat breakfast, shower, and go to the command bunker to see if my orders had arrived. I hadn't written a letter in more than two months. I didn't want to talk about what I was experiencing; I couldn't focus. I felt guilty. I knew my loved ones were frantic wondering if I was okay. Finally, on days fifteen and fourteen, I wrote letters to my mom, dad, my two sisters, and three girlfriends even though I agonized over where to start and what to say.

The letters that I got from Mom and Dad kept me informed on what was happening with the relatives and the community. Letters from my sisters brought me up to speed on friends and gossip. The girlfriend letters were exciting. They offered hope, intimacy, and something to fantasize about. I had been officially relieved of my duties, and it felt great.

GIs were allowed to send all their personal possessions home before they flew out. Supply, the Army Walmart, gave each of us a footlocker. It was a one-foot-by-two-foot-by-three-foot plywood box.

It took all of day thirteen to go through my gear and pack it in my footlocker. It felt good to be doing things for the last time.

THE SHADOW OF DEATH

I had been taking two showers a day. Every shower washed more red dirt out of my pores. It almost looked like blood. When you're in the field, the only shower you get is from the rain. During the dry season, it doesn't rain, and it's over one hundred degrees every day. The dust is choking. It stuck to sweat-soaked skin, and the heat would bake it into your body. It was almost a month before it stopped.

There were five of us short timers who were all waiting for our orders. The orders were typed and came in from headquarters in Saigon with our dates of rotation back to the states. Everything came into us by chopper, so every time one came in, we got excited. Every night, the five of us got together after evening chow. We'd play basketball or touch football until it got dark. Then we'd shower and play double deck pinochle and drink beer. It was great because we hadn't had many relaxing moments.

The first of us to go was Specialist 5th Class Smearman. He was the company clerk and was from Pittsburgh, Pennsylvania. His job was prestigious, like being an executive secretary. He handled all the paperwork for the battalion. He always knew what was going on, and those of us he liked he kept informed. The best part of his job was that he never left base camp and he had never been in combat. Most combat soldiers had spent fewer than three weeks total in base camp.

That day, he turned in his weapon, an M16. We kidded him because it had never been fired. He had a going away party for himself that night. He had a bottle of good Bourbon and several cases of beer. The beer had been iced down in trash cans. Ice and American beer were two things that were hard to come by in Vietnam.

We played cards and talked about what would be the first thing we would do when we got home. My firsts would be Grandma's pan-fried chicken, mashed potatoes and gravy, and a garden salad. I would get a hand-squeezed cherry limeade from the Dairy Plaza down on the corner that was run by two old ladies. I'd want a deep wet kiss from one of the prettiest girls in town and a beer keg party down on the Arkansas River with a sandy beach, crystal clear water, a big bonfire, and pretty girls in swimsuits. They all sounded great but probably wouldn't be in that order. My first night back in base camp, we had a going away party for Smearman. He was our company clerk, and he was flying home the next day. His year in Vietnam was up.

I never liked any kind of hard liquor, but the ice cold beer tasted good. It numbed my brain. We had been playing cards for three hours, and I didn't want any more beer. Smearman noticed that I had stopped drinking. He asked why, and I told him that I had maxed out.

"I got something else that works," he said. He left and returned with a joint, the size of a cigar.

Some people in the states had a perception that most of the Vietnam soldiers were into drugs. I never saw any hard drugs the year I was there. I never even heard anybody talk about hard drugs. Pot was easy to get, and most of the villages we went through had several people trying to sell it to the GIs.

Almost every platoon had two or three guys smoking it. But those who partook were careful when and where they used it. Some officers and sergeants looked the other way, while others were hard asses and would report you. But using in the field, out of base camp, or in combat was not tolerated and would get you in big trouble.

In the battalion I was in, most of the guys knew little or nothing about pot. The kicker was that the Californians were experts on pot and they educated the other soldiers on it. In our battalion, all of our medics were from California. One of the medics was due to rotate home four days ahead of me. He was from California like the other medics.

The rumor was that instead of putting his personal belongings in his footlocker, he bought pot in the village to fill his footlocker. He said that if his footlocker cleared military customs, he would be a rich man. Whether he ended up rich or in a federal penitentiary, we never heard.

Smearman knew that I didn't mess with drugs. He lit the joint, took a hit, and offered it to me. I declined it. He pressured me.

"Come on, man," he said. "It's my last night."

I finally took a hit. I was too mentally worn out to keep arguing. During the following half hour, I took a couple more hits and then left to go to my hooch and sleep.

THE SHADOW OF DEATH

In the year I spent in Vietnam, I had tried marijuana one other time. It was right after a battle. I was exhausted, but for some reason, I couldn't sleep. The temperature topped 110 degrees. My eyes were blood shot and burning, and I was soaked in sweat. There was no place to get a shower. I needed water bad, but I didn't have the strength to move. We were sitting on the ground with our backs leaning against my track.

The soldier next to me was Sergeant Chuck Johnson. Chuck was from St. Paul, Minnesota. He was the TC on Romeo 24. This was the track next to mine on my right flank when we were in a combat formation. He reached into his shirt pocket, pulled out a joint, lit it, took a hit off it, and passed it to me. He told me what to do. I took a hit off it and passed it back to him. My first impression was that it was like the first time you take a drug on a cigarette. The tobacco was harsh on my throat, and I felt light-headed. This time, I held the smoke in my lungs like he told me to. Finally, I coughed out the smoke. We talked for a few minutes. Gradually, my eyelids got heavy, and I drifted away to sleep.

That was what I expected to happen the second time. I laid down on my cot thinking that I was going to drift away into a grateful sleep.

We slept on Army cots in base camp canvas beds two feet off the ground that were hard as concrete. I had an air mattress on top of mine. I had a one-inch wooden framework around the sides and on top of it with mosquito netting covering the frame. I had a sleeping bag on top of the air mattress. I kept a razor sharp bayonet tucked under my sleeping bag in case of emergency. Sleeping with a loaded rifle was more dangerous than the enemy. I tucked the mosquito netting under the mattress all the way around. It kept the snakes and the bugs out.

All of a sudden, I felt like I was floating, and I could see myself floating off my cot and drifting toward the moon. I quickly grabbed the sides of my cot and pulled myself back on top of my sleeping bag. I couldn't let go or I would start to float off my cot again. Next, I thought I was in the dessert dying of thirst. That was the last thing I remembered. The next morning, I woke up under a lister. It was a rubber bladder shaped like a fifty-gallon cylinder full of drinking water. I woke up lying on my back underneath one of the faucets, and my stomach hurt terribly. I looked down at my stomach, and it looked as though it was going to explode. Thinking that I was dying of thirst, I had drunk way too much water.

Smearman was gone, and a new day had started.

Chapter 16

The sergeant major told me that he needed me at the command bunker at 4 p.m. When I got there, he told me that two officers and a buck sergeant were flying in from Bravo Company. They were going to court martial, the sergeant who had assaulted his platoon leader and company commander. He was in big trouble. I was told Bravo Company had returned to base camp after being in combat for sixty days. The first night back in base camp, everyone was allowed to let their hair down and get drunk. You can even get away with a little hell-raising. But you can't get drunk and beat up two senior officers in the company.

When they brought him in, the sergeant was shackled hands and feet. I knew him. His name was Hardesty. We had gone to recon school together in Fort Knox, Kentucky. He was from the hills of West Virginia. He was a good guy, and I felt sorry for him. He had fewer than thirty days left in country, and now he was looking at ten years in a military prison.

The sergeant major signed him over to me. I took possession of the prisoner. He was my responsibility until midnight. After a while, there were just my two runners and me in the Headquarters Command bunker. We started talking, and he knew that he was in deep shit. I could tell by our conversation that mentally he wasn't right.

He asked me if he had any mail. He was married and hoping for a letter from his wife. I found three letters for him, and they were indeed from his wife. He started reading the letters and tears started to flow. He told me how much his wife loved him. He wanted me to read one of the letters so that I would know just how much she loved him. I told him that I believed him and that I didn't want to read his personal letters. But he insisted. I finally did just to make him happy, and I told him what a lucky man he was.

He told me that he had to go to the bathroom and asked me to take him. I asked him if I could trust him, and he said, "Yes." I removed his shackles and told him to go straight to the latrine and to come straight back. But then I got involved in other things and forgot about him. Curious, I got up from the front desk to look for him, and he came through the door with an M16 rifle that he had taken from another soldier. It was pointed at my chest, and he told me that he would kill me if I didn't do what he said. My weapon was in a corner too far away. I was screwed.

The two officers who were going to testify against him were going to come back to the command bunker. Hardesty said that he was going to kill them both and then himself. He wasn't going to prison for ten years, he said.

We sat and waited for the officers to return. All the while, I was trying to talk him out of it. He wasn't listening. Finally, he got tired of waiting and ordered me to go outside the bunker with him. He was going to shoot them when they pulled up in the jeep. I was still trying to talk him out of it.

I knew that I had to do something. He was my prisoner, and I had let him get away. In military law, I was responsible for his actions. We would receive the same sentence. I knew that I had to try and take the weapon away from him. I looked into his eyes, and he must have read my mind.

"Try it, and I will kill you," he said.

I stood there trying to figure out what to do. Finally, he got tired of waiting for the two officers. He got into the jeep that was parked in front of the command bunker. He was going to drive to the part of our compound where the officers were and shoot them.

To get where he had to go, he had to drive in the opposite direction before the road turned back the way he wanted to go. He left me standing there in front of the command bunker. When he had turned the jeep around and headed away from me, I took off on a dead run to the area where the officers were. I hoped I could get there ahead of him because I was cutting straight across our compound.

When I got to the maintenance area where the officers were, they were standing on a new tank. I screamed at them to get inside the tank and button up. Sergeant Hardesty had gotten away from me and was on his way there to kill them. They had just locked inside the tank when Hardesty arrived and walked around the back side of the tank toward me. He had the M16 pointed at my chest. He knew that I had just screwed up his plan. I thought I was a dead man.

I started talking to him, telling him that his wife needed him and about some of the things she said in her letters.

There were some other soldiers there, but when they saw Hardesty, they all ran except for one. While I was talking to Hardesty, a soldier whose name I never knew slowly and cautiously came up behind the sergeant. Hardesty had the M16 at his waist. The soldier struck down hard on the stock of the M16. Hardesty pulled the trigger, but all of the bullets went over my left shoulder. The soldier reached over the top of Hardesty's shoulder and grabbed the rifle barrel. I jumped on the sergeant, and between the soldier and myself, we took the weapon away from him. I sent a man to the command bunker to get the shackles. I put them on him, and he was back in my custody.

That afternoon, Hardesty was court marshaled. He got twenty years in Leavenworth Prison. I had to testify against him. I no longer felt sorry for him, but I did feel sorry for his wife back home who loved him. And me, I had a new best friend. He saved my life.

Six days left.

Chapter 17

The day after Sergeant Hardesty's court martial, I was still going over the events. I felt sorry for him because life as he knew it had just come to an end. I knew that he would have murdered the two officers, and he would have killed me too, if I had not gotten lucky. He had snapped. He couldn't take the stress anymore, either mentally or physically.

That night, Sergeant Bergin, three new recon recruits, and I were playing poker in my hooch. When new soldiers came in, they had to go through a week of indoctrination before they were sent into combat. They had one-hour classes on weapons, explosives, booby traps, venereal diseases, malaria, and you name it. We would ask them about what was going on back home. It was nice to know that the rest of the world was still there. Things were going great. We were laughing and joking and taking all the recruits' money. They weren't going to need it where they were going.

All of a sudden, I heard this faint whistle. I knew immediately that it was a 105 rocket. Sergeant Bergin and I jumped up and made a mad scramble for the door. The problem was that the new recruits were between us and the door. We were pushing, shoving, and screaming to get outside in the trenches. I was the second one through the door. The recruit who was ahead of me was pushed out of my way as I dove into the trench.

Outside of our hooch, we had a four-by-four-by-four latrine. It had about three feet of urine in it. When I pushed the recruit, he went in head first. We had all made it into the trenches, and nobody got hurt. We were laughing because we could hear the recruit spitting and sputtering and swearing. The ground was shaking from the rocket attack, and the new recruit was too scared to move.

I didn't get much sleep that night.

The next morning, I got up, got dressed, and headed for the mess tent for breakfast. The walk there reminded me of the surface of the moon. There were craters everywhere from the rocket attack. It was a reminder that death was everywhere in this place.

Sergeant Bergin was down to two days left in country. I had four. We were the last men left standing out of the original forty-four men in our recon platoon. Four of us had made it. The other two had already headed home.

Sergeant Bergin was raised on the streets of New York. He was tough, hard core. He was a good soldier. The word gentleman was not a word that registered in his mind. He was a survivor. He came over to my hooch just about every night for the last twenty days. We'd play cards, laugh about a few things, reminisce about others, and drink a few cold beers. This was like a resort compared to what we had been through. I guess we understood each other. We helped each other pass the time until our departure dates.

I respected him, but I didn't like him. We were different men, and we both knew it. He was a career soldier, and I was a three-year man. But our main differences were morals and character. An incident that night would show how.

We had just finished evening chow, and I went back to my hooch, got out of my fatigues, wrapped a towel around me, put on my flip-flops, and headed for the shower. I finished my shower and headed back to my hooch. Tim Raney was the new company clerk, replacing Smearman. Raney was from Dallas, Texas. The city fit his ego. He thought he was God's gift to women. The irony was that he hadn't been in country but a month when he got a Dear John letter from his wife.

Danny McCoin was a jeep driver for the company commander. He was from Paris, Texas. He was a big old raw-boned country boy. He had a great sense of humor and was a lousy poker player, two traits I admired.

Charles Tojas was my replacement and was going through indoctrination. He was from Syracuse, New York. He was a newlywed and spent every spare minute writing letters home to his wife. I knew he was going to have a tough time. He was really homesick and missed his wife terribly.

The last soldier was Jim Lawless. He had been a used-car salesman in Houston, Texas. He was working in S-4 which was logistics. He was the most sarcastic man I had ever met, and he was constantly getting his ass whipped.

But back to Bergin, he came through the door and passed by all of those guys while I was sitting there relaxing. He came toward me, and I saw that he was clearly drunk. When he was a couple of steps away from me, he stopped and looked at me.

"You son of a bitch." Then he turned and walked out of the hooch.

What I didn't know—and didn't find out until late—was that when he was walking past the other guys, one of them had called him a "dumb fucking wop." He was so drunk that he thought that I had said it.

Bergin announced his return by kicking the door open and screaming my name. He had found an M16 somewhere; he had already checked his weapon in because he was leaving the next day. He was halfway to me when he opened fire. I was still in my towel and shower shoes. I dove through the mosquito netting and out through the tent.

The barracks we were living in were twenty feet wide and forty feet long. They had wooden frames and a wooden floor. A fitted military tent was thrown over the top of them. On the outside, they had a sandbag wall up against the canvas all the way around the barracks. The wall was four feet high and would protect the sleeping soldiers from mortar and rocket attacks. On the inside of the barracks, the walls were eight feet tall. From the floor up, the first four feet was solid wall. The next four feet was all mosquito netting. The other men in the barracks were all diving out too. I don't know if he could see us in the darkness or if he was unsure who to shoot.

When I dove through the screen, I hit and rolled. I jumped up and took off on a dead run straight away from the hooch. There was a water tanker some one hundred yards away. I headed for it. I wanted to get to the tanker where I could see back to my hooch and yet still have a big piece of equipment between Bergin and me. I assessed my situation. I had kicked off my shower shoes so I could run. I was barefoot, had a towel wrapped around me, and had no weapon. I moved away from my barracks to another area of the compound. I went to three different barracks before I got everything I needed. Then, I headed back for my barracks. I was scratched up, embarrassed, and pissed off. I got to the tanker I climbed up on it so I could see. When I was running and hiding, I heard gunfire a couple of times. I didn't know if Bergin had shot someone or gotten himself shot. I was hoping for the latter.

I stayed on the tanker until daylight. I had a good field of vision and a lot of protection. About an hour after daylight, I saw Danny McCoin going into our barracks, and I hollered at him. He came over to the tanker and told me that no one had been killed or wounded, including Bergin. He had missed everyone in our barracks. He went into the other two barracks and emptied a clip into the roof of both of them. He then went to the mess hall, shot the lock off of the door, and made a midnight snack. He passed out there. They got his weapon while he was sleeping and put the handcuffs on him. They woke him and took him to the command bunker and handcuffed him to the bumper of the jeep.

I walked to our barracks with McCoin. We went inside and saw that everything had been shot up. I told McCoin that I was leaving the next day, but if I had any more time than that, I'd have gone back into combat. At least I knew who my enemies were out there. He laughed. He told me that it was Lawless who had insulted Bergin.

I went over to the command bunker where Bergin was indeed handcuffed to the bumper of a jeep. I walked up to the sergeant major who asked me if I was okay. I told him I was fine. The sergeant major asked me where I got the M16. I told him Charley Company. If it was all the same to him, I said, I would hang onto it until the next morning.

As we approached Bergin, I asked the sergeant major what they would do with him. He said they hadn't made up their minds whether they were going to court martial him or put him on the next chopper out and let him go home.

Bergin was lying in the dirt. He looked pathetic. He was hungover and he looked it. He looked at me and said that he was sorry.

"You're right," I said and walked away.

Back at my hooch, I checked my uniform for bullet holes. I was tired. I had been up all night, but I couldn't go to sleep. I grabbed a towel and my M16 and headed for the shower. After my shower, I headed for the mess hall to get something to eat. The sergeant major came to my table and told me that Bergin was on a chopper and on his way home. He was a career soldier, so they decided to cut him some slack.

In fewer than twenty-four hours, I would be out of here. I decided to try to get some sleep.

That afternoon I cleaned the brass on my uniform and polished my boots for the twentieth time. I allowed myself to think about my loved ones, my home, and what I was going to do when I got there. I didn't sleep that night. I heard every sound. I got up early and took a shower. I put on my dress khakis. I went to the mess hall for several cups of black coffee and then headed over to the command bunker. I said my goodbyes.

I asked the sergeant major if the chopper pilot could stop in Chu Lai. It was on our way to Saigon, and three men from our platoon were in the hospital there. He took me to the chopper pad and told me he was happy for me.

I saluted him and walked away. I couldn't talk; I was too emotional.

I got in the chopper, and we took off. It was like a dream. I had fantasized about this day for three hundred sixty four days. I looked at the land below and wondered if I could ever put this all behind me. My thoughts drifted back to my dead friends. Somehow, I felt like I was abandoning them. I made myself promise that I would try to contact their families.

THE SHADOW OF DEATH

We landed on the medevac pad at the hospital. I went inside and immediately had an uneasy feeling. There was the same sickening sweet smell in this hospital as there had been in the two that I had been in. The nurses were American girls. They looked beautiful.

I went to see Liccione first. He was from Chicago and had been a driver on my recon track. A bullet had cut a path through the side of his face. He had several stitches, but he was okay. He asked me if anybody had broken his record. He had the record for the most venereal diseases in our company. I laughed, and we talked for a while. He was happy for me, and I knew that I gave him hope.

I said goodbye. He had been my fourth driver. The other three hadn't been so lucky.

The next was Grabowski. He was a kid from the south side of Milwaukee and had been a gunner on my track. An RPG hit the gun shield on his machine gun, and the shrapnel went into his face. The nurse took me to see him. His face was swollen twice its normal size. His eyes were slits, and the tip of his nose was gone. He was so doped up that I didn't know if he even knew I was there. I held his hand and talked to him for a while.

I said goodbye and left.

The last was Private Luke. He was from a small town outside of Baton Rouge, Louisiana. I really liked him. We had been in a major battle together. We had pulled back and called in for artillery support. He was standing out in front of the track. The artillery came in on top of us instead of on top of the enemy. Shrapnel from one of the rounds hit him in the groin. The nurse took me to him.

As I approached, he recognized me and started to cry. I sat down alongside of him and asked what was bothering him. He told me that he had lost his genitals in the attack. His testicles and penis were gone. He asked me what I thought his wife would do. They had been married for only four months when he was shipped to Vietnam. I told him if she really loved him, it wouldn't matter. We talked for a while longer. I got him to laugh, and then I said goodbye to him too.

I went back to the helicopter, and we took off for Saigon. I promised myself that I would never again go into another field hospital.

Chapter 18

Home

The field hospital jeep took me back to the chopper pad. The Huey lifted up and away. We followed the ocean shoreline to Saigon. I was looking at the beaches and the waves rolling in. In one area, I could see swimmers in the water; and close by, there were a dozen small sharks swimming close to them. It reminded me that no matter where you were in this country, death was always close by.

We flew over Vung Toa. It was a beach resort that our military had built for the GIs. During a one-year tour of duty, you were allowed one seven-day out-of-country R&R and one four-day in-country R&R. The only place to go in-country was Vung Toa. All the soldiers I knew who came back from four days there said that it consisted of a big beach, unlimited cheap alcohol, and government-controlled and government-inspected prostitutes.

I never took either an in-country or an out-of-country R&R.

The year I spent in Vietnam, I never touched a woman. I had the satisfaction of knowing that I had left nothing behind that was part of me. The resort below never touched me.

I'm not a saint, far from it. But to be intimate with a stranger for money, even lonely, unhappy, and in serious need of tender loving care was something I couldn't do.

It was hard for me to look down on Vung Toa and get my mind around this. We profess to be a Christian nation fighting the evils of Communism for the South Vietnamese. But then we turn their women into prostitutes to keep the troops happy? It diminished my opinion of my country. It embarrassed and sickened me. Where did the white knight in shining armor go? When and how did we lose our way? Where were our leaders' morals and convictions?

As Vung Toa faded behind me, I looked ahead for Saigon in the distance. I found it almost impossible to sleep. It had been four days since I had slept more than three hours. Now, I was too afraid to even take a nap. I was afraid that I would wake up back in the jungle.

We touched down in Saigon. One of my friends was a liaison to a general there. The general had arranged it so that I could fly back to the states on an Air Force C-130. I had forty minutes to catch that flight. My friend took me to the plane in his jeep. We had time for only a short conversation, but it brought me back to reality and I needed that. I grabbed my duffle bag and walked to the plane.

A C-130 is loaded from the back of the plane. One of the crew members took me inside to the front of the plane. My seat fell down from the wall. It was a green nylon chair. It was uncomfortable, but I didn't care. One of the crew told me that they were almost loaded and we'd be taking off in twenty minutes. I looked at the ceiling and drifted off into my thoughts. The next thing I knew, we were taxiing down the runway. I felt the plane leave the ground and slowly start to bank away from the airport. I looked out the window and saw that we were leaving land and headed out over the ocean.

I finally drifted off into a fitful sleep. I woke up about four hours later. Reality hit me for the first time—I was really going home. I had left Vietnam never to return, and it was almost overwhelming.

My eyes began to focus on the cargo. It was row after row of stainless steel boxes. I hadn't noticed them when I boarded the plane. One of the crew walked by, and I asked him what they were. They were caskets with dead GI's bodies inside, he said.

I was shocked at first, and I later wondered if any of my friends were in them. Suddenly, a feeling of relief came over me because I knew that they were going home too. They would never tell their loved ones about what happened in Vietnam, and neither would I.

Some ten years after the Vietnam War was over, Ho Chi Men, the leader of North Vietnam, said had the United States fought for one more day, they would have sued for peace.

About the Author

KURT A. VOMBERG is a freelance writer. The *Shadow of Death* is his first published book, and he worked on it for over eight years! Kurt was born in Dodge City, KS, and was raised in nearby Kinsley, KS. He graduated from Kinsley High School in 1963. After attending and graduating from Dodge City Junior College, he enlisted in the military and served from 1966 to 1969.

He proudly served in the United States Army and went to Vietnam for a one-year tour of duty. During that time, Kurt was in A Company, 1st and the 12th, 1st Calvary Division and then Headquarters Company, 2nd and 34th, Armored Division.

Kurt's recon platoon began with a total of forty-four men of which only four survived to complete their one-year tour of duty. Upon his return to the United States, Kurt was decorated by Two-Star General Shae at Fort Hood, Texas.

After completing his military commitment, Kurt attended Marquette University where he graduated with a bachelor's degree in business in 1972.

He enjoys spending time on his ranch in Bristow, Oklahoma. Kurt's started out to write a book that would help show the American people what so many brave men went through during the Vietnam War. It was never meant to be about him but to tell the story for so many whose voices were silenced! He also wanted to show young people who are contemplating a military career that war is never glamorous and it remains with you for a lifetime!